GRASPING THE RING

Nine Unique Winners in Life and Sports

By Gene A. Budig

With foreword by
Bob Costas

Published by
The News-Gazette, Inc.

The News-Gazette®

EDITOR AND PUBLISHER | John Foreman
PROJECT EDITOR | Amy Eckert
ART DIRECTOR | Joan Millis

Cover design and book layout: Joan Millis, The News-Gazette

Soft cover ISBN: 978-0-9798420-3-0

© 2008 by The News-Gazette, Inc.

Printed in the United States of America

The News-Gazette, Inc.
15 Main Street
Champaign, IL 61820
Phone: (217) 351-5252
Fax: (217) 351-5245
www.news-gazette.com

To Gretchen, Christopher,
Mary Frances and Kathryn

All of the proceeds from the sale
of this book that are due the author will go
to CollegeEd, an innovative program
designed by the College Board
to increase the number of deserving
young people who attend college.

CONTENTS

FOREWORD
by Bob Costas

In the following pages, Professor Gene A. Budig provides telling insights about a series of exceptional people who have been driven to lead and to excel on the national stage. He knows each person very well and points to their strengths, and a few weaknesses. Regardless of your view of them, they are all compelling personalities.

Former U. S. Senators Bob Dole and Bob Kerrey were heroes in World War II and Vietnam, respectively, and each carried the crippling wounds of war as they went on to impact national policy as political leaders.

Hall of Fame coaches Tom Osborne and Roy Williams achieved the ultimate in college football and basketball; Osborne winning national championships on the gridiron at Nebraska, and Williams doing the same on the hardwood at Chapel Hill.

With dogged determination and unusual creativity, Al Neuharth founded USA TODAY, the country's most widely read newspaper. He proved that American ingenuity was alive and well, and he beat the odds with finesse and flare.

George Steinbrenner is an original, buying the New York Yankees in 1973 for $8.7 million, and turning them into a perennial winner and a sports enterprise today valued at nearly two billion dollars. Many managers and players have been toppled in his wake, but the bottom line shows him with ten American League pennants and six World Series championships.

Another American success story is Jerry Reinsdorf, a kid from Brooklyn who went on to become a lawyer, public accountant, real estate developer, and eventually the owner of the Chicago White Sox and the Chicago Bulls. He has seven coveted world championship rings; one from the 2005 White

Sox, and six from the Bulls and Michael Jordan during the 1990s.

Two of Dr. Budig's most engaging and moving chapters deal with football great Gale Sayers of the University of Kansas and the Chicago Bears, and Larry Doby, the first African American to break the color barrier in the American League.

Sayers shattered numerous records as an elusive running back and punt returner with the Jayhawks and the Bears during his Hall of Fame career. Some still say he was the game's greatest broken field runner, and he is remembered on virtually every all-time National Football League team.

Doby broke into big league baseball in 1947 with the Cleveland Indians, just 11 weeks after Jackie Robinson donned a Brooklyn Dodgers uniform. In his 13-year Hall of Fame career, Doby hit .283 with 253 home runs, 1,515 hits, and 970 runs batted in. He played on seven consecutive American League All Star teams.

Dr. Budig has had a long and remarkable career himself, serving as the President/Chancellor at three major state universities (Illinois State University, West Virginia University, and the University of Kansas), as the past President of Major League Baseball's American League, and as a professor at five universities, including the University of Nebraska-Lincoln and Princeton University. He is a retired major general in the Air National Guard/United States Air Force.

Despite these impressive achievements, I have always found Gene to be an unassuming and self-effacing man. It is typical of him to be so genuinely interested in the stories and perspectives of others.

Bob Costas
NBC and HBO Sports

INTRODUCTION

Over a span of 35 years, I have been fortunate to meet, converse with, and introduce many interesting people, some of whom have been seen on the front pages of America's newspapers and on evening news telecasts.

Presidents of the United States, senators and representatives, governors, members of the Supreme Court, and international dignitaries have passed my way because of the institutions that I have been blessed to represent.

Other notable visitors to the University of Nebraska, Illinois State University, West Virginia University, the University of Kansas, and the 30 ballparks of Major League Baseball have included high-profile titans from business and industry, college and university presidents, labor leaders, journalists, Nobel laureates and Pulitzer Prize winners, distinguished professors and outstanding teachers, and television and movie personalities, among others.

Most of them have had timely and challenging substance to offer, especially to eager, impressionable young college students. Experience from elders, with graying or no hair, has its value especially in this ever-changing and uncertain world.

Among the long parade of intriguing people, I have singled out nine of them; each was compelling, but in a different way. No two were alike. Each had unshakable values, some of which were hard to understand and appreciate, and each dared to confront overwhelming odds to make a real difference and, though not his purpose, to gain a unique place in American history.

Each was, at times, complex and private, and each delivered a message of hope and strength. Some were humble; others were not. Some were more likable than others. Admittedly, many more people could have been chosen; certainly, no slight is intended.

The selectees are George M. Steinbrenner, Larry Doby, Tom

Osborne, Roy Williams, Gale Sayers, Jerry Reinsdorf, Bob Kerrey, Al Neuharth, and Bob Dole. They are very different individuals, yet they share certain values and traits, ones that engender public notice, interest, respect, and sometimes irritation. They have enormous strengths and some very visible warts. They are, after all, human.

I have known each of them for a considerable length of time, and each was responsive to my questions and comments. Some were more patient than others. They rightfully questioned a few of my conclusions, as I thought they would. Each has added to my understanding, and it was especially moving when Larry Doby and Coach Williams remembered me in their acceptance speeches to Halls of Fame in recent years.

The people featured in this book did not seek attention; in truth, they did me and the readers a favor. They widened our horizons on a number of pressing and timeless issues, on ways to experience inner satisfaction. They were, above all, candid.

More than 100 people helped me gather information on these subjects, and offered thoughtful and relevant interpretations of the findings. Their contributions were essential. Fairness and objectivity were paramount throughout the involved process, which took nearly three years to accomplish. Those who gave a hand included newspaper reporters and columnists, politicians, college coaches, past and current baseball players, managers and owners, academics, publishers, family members and friends of the nine, and more than a few critics.

Importantly, all evoked heartfelt emotions regardless of differing takes on matters.

Gene A. Budig

a Yankee
Doodle Dandy

George M. Steinbrenner, the sometimes reviled owner of the New York Yankees, has arguably done more than anyone else to keep baseball energized and visible to growing numbers of fans from across the country. His influence reaches far beyond the gates of historic Yankee Stadium in the Bronx.

He has built a team that helps maintain the spotlight on Major League Baseball in an increasingly competitive sports and entertainment environment. More than 78 million men, women, and children passed through turnstiles in 2007 to cheer on their favorite major league teams, setting an attendance record for the fourth consecutive year.

The Yankees easily outdrew the other 29 MLB clubs. Owners love having the Bronx Bombers come to town because those games result in much larger than usual crowds and spirited competition. No team draws better on the road than the Yanks, and that has been true for generations. Derek Jeter, the team captain, once told me that he is energized by the chorus of boos that greet him and his teammates outside of New York.

Nearly 43 million more people witnessed minor league games in 2007, setting a record for the fifth straight year. The farm teams of the Yankees were especially successful at the gate and on the field.

Commissioner of Baseball Bud Selig takes justifiable pride in the fact that his sport posted an attendance figure that will be larger

The Boss

George M. Steinbrenner at historic Yankee Stadium.

than the combined ticket sales of the National Football League, the National Basketball Association, and the National Hockey League. And that does not include the totals from the flourishing minor leagues. Baseball remains America's pastime and, in truth, the game has never been more popular.

Selig and Steinbrenner agree that the reasons for the continuing surge in popularity are the wild card, interleague play, increased balance among teams because of economic reforms, and the construction and preservation of fan-friendly ballparks. Nearly two-thirds of the major league clubs were in contention for playoffs as late as Labor Day and, clearly, there has never been greater competitive balance.

The Yankees write large checks for MLB revenue sharing and the so-called luxury tax, monies that find their way to other clubs, and Steinbrenner often grumbles about it. He believes the current system of revenue distribution is grossly unfair to his Yankees and advantages clubs that do not use the funds for the intended purpose—player improvement. The original intent was for a system that would enhance the quality of the on-field product for those people who buy the millions of tickets.

George Steinbrenner freely admits to being headstrong at times, always an entrepreneur, and an unflinching patriot. He has systematically built the Yankees into the most storied franchise in all of sports, and into a multi-billion-dollar enterprise that is not for sale. The Yankees will have a new ballpark in 2009 that some already believe will be referred to as "The House that Steinbrenner Built." The old stadium is often called "The House that Ruth Built."

The Yankees will account for a significant part of the more than $5.5 billion that MLB will generate in 2008, and that figure will be a record too.

One needs to understand that Steinbrenner is, first and

foremost, determined and rarely deterred. He always seeks a competitive edge for his players, and he regularly questions umpiring calls that go against them. In my first season, he invited me to sit with him during a game at the stadium. He never let up on the umpiring crew, and he asked what I intended to do to straighten out umpires. "This can't go on," he kept bellowing before two of his assistants came to my rescue and changed the subject. As the rookie league president, I left my two hot dogs and soda untouched.

The Yankees belong to the Steinbrenner family, and that will not change anytime soon. The principal owner believes owning the Yankees is much like possessing a rare piece of art, and such masterpieces are meant to be enjoyed, not sold. Without question, there would be a long line of suitors with deep pockets if the team was ever put up for sale.

"The team has brought millions of people years of lasting joy, and I count myself among them," Steinbrenner told me early in 2007. "I do what I have to do to protect its past and guarantee its future. Yankees fans in the city of New York and elsewhere deserve a winner, year in and year out."

The Yankee faithful, and there are untold numbers of them most everywhere, love to hate Steinbrenner at times. His decisions are often controversial, greeted with outcry from the sports pages of New York and on the subways of the city. Everyone, it seems, knows what is best for the New York Yankees. A true Yankee fan delights in second guessing the owner, especially on player personnel decisions.

At the same time, the die-hard New York baseball fans know that George Steinbrenner will spend whatever it takes to win. His player payroll exceeded $200 million in 2007, easily the highest in all of Major League Baseball. The World Series Champion Boston Red Sox expended less than $150 million. Steinbrenner defends his payroll, without hesitation, as a needed and expected expenditure in New York. "You have to be willing to spend to win," he once told me at an owners meeting.

The rarely deterred owner reminded me more than once during my six years as American League president that "winning is the most important thing in my life, after breathing. Breathing first, winning second." He has always sought a competitive advantage, explaining that the people of New York deserve no less from the owner of the Yankees.

My first face-to-face encounter with the Boss came during my third day in office. He stormed in unannounced, refused to take a chair, and declared that he had never liked AL presidents and he felt that would be the case with me. "You're obviously overqualified for the job; you're a college president," he asserted. The meeting lasted no more than five minutes, and on the way out he paused to tell one of my associates that "Dr. Budig got the message."

Like the league presidents before me, I was one of his favorite targets and I often felt the sting of his biting public criticism. My predecessors, Lee MacPhail and Dr. Bobby Brown, warned me about Steinbrenner and his tirades during the playing season. Baseball executives in New York had reason to be cautious in their dealings with him and his subordinates.

MacPhail was elected to the Baseball Hall of Fame in 1998, joining his father Larry, who had been elected in 1978. They are the first father-and-son members. Lee, one of the game's most respected gentlemen, once served as general manager of the New York Yankees. His son Andy is currently the CEO of the Baltimore Orioles.

Brown, a man of letters with a medical degree from Tulane University, played 548 regular season games for the Yankees with a lifetime batting average of .279. He played in four World Series

(1947, 1949, 1950, 1951) for New York, batting .439 in 17 games. His road roommate was Yogi Berra.

Lee and Bobby were trusted advisers to me throughout my tenure as league president; they were able professionals who clearly understood the game and especially what it took to deal with the bigger-than-life Yankees.

I struck a nerve during the summer of 2007 by writing a commentary essay for the Associated Press that called for the selection of Steinbrenner to the Baseball Hall of Fame at Cooperstown. A few of my former associates in New York were annoyed by the article, but the overall response was quite positive. I am even more convinced today that he has earned a place beside fellow pinstripers Ruth, Gehrig, DiMaggio, Mantle, Berra, Jackson, Ford, and Rizzuto, among others.

It does not matter whether you revere him, as many do on the streets of New York, or resent him, as many do in other major league cities. His record of success is indisputable. During his more than 30 stormy years in the Bronx, his Yankees have won ten American League pennants and six World Championships. No team has done better in either league. In fact, no team has even come close.

I have dealt with Steinbrenner and his moods on numerous occasions, and I found him to be at least two people—one driven by ambition and emotion, the other generous to a fault. He has never met a worthy cause that he was unwilling to support. He has been extremely generous to charities in New York and Tampa, Florida, where he and his family reside. Without question, he is complex and hard to understand at times.

I saw a different side of him when the University of Kansas opened its largest classroom facility, bearing my name, in October 1997. Without any announcement, he chartered a private jet and flew from Tampa to Lawrence for the ceremony. He talked to everyone in sight, signed numerous autographs, and smiled for photos with the baseball fans in attendance. He even told the governor that I was doing a commendable job for the American League.

There is no doubt that Steinbrenner can be difficult to work for and with. He changed managers 20 times in his first 23 seasons, and five times he hired and fired the temperamental Billy Martin. More than a few of his former managers and general managers remained on the payroll, in one role or another. He liked most of them and their families, and he especially admired Hall of Famers Bob Lemon and Yogi Berra. He hired Joe Torre as his manager in 1995, and that relationship endured for a dozen years and four World Series titles.

Their parting was painful to witness, especially for the people closest to them. I, for one, like and respect both of them. Steinbrenner made Torre a rich man and a certainty for election to the Hall of Fame. George and his sons Hank and Hal appreciated what Joe had achieved during his years as manager, but the Yankees had not won a World Series in seven years. That was an eternity to George and he did not believe it was good enough for the fans of New York, especially since the Yankees were preparing for a new ballpark. Joe, on the other hand, felt a one-year contract extension was an affront since he had led his teams to the postseason for 12 consecutive seasons. The controversial split was not about money; it was about pride.

Once at a league meeting, George said he would never suffer a heart attack, adding that he only gives them. He also reminded his 11 general managers of that contention and in those few words. He was being dead serious.

Steinbrenner was suspended twice from baseball, but each time he returned with renewed zeal to win on the field. He rarely talks about the past; it seems to bore him. He prefers to talk about the future and what it will take for the Yankees to win it all. Some around the game regard him as a bully, while others, and especially the Yankee faithful, see him as a champion who will spend what it takes to win.

The Cleveland native is, without question, a highly successful entrepreneur who can sound more like a college football coach than an owner of a sports empire. Legendary coach Woody Hayes of Ohio State was one of Steinbrenner's all-time favorites. A student athlete at Williams College, Steinbrenner began a brief career in coaching as a football assistant at Northwestern and Purdue. He was driven by his father to succeed at both athletics and business.

Times change, and people change. For example, Steinbrenner now considers me and Bill White to be his two all-time favorite league presidents. White was an all-star first baseman for the St. Louis Cardinals, an announcer for Yankee games on television, and president of the National League. "You two had character and baseball needs guys like you," he told me recently, as he has told his staff.

Perhaps Don Walton, a veteran columnist for the Lincoln (NE) Journal and Star, said it best when he wrote, "Major League Baseball is more than the Yankees, but it would be a lot less without them."

There is considerable speculation about the health of Mr. Steinbrenner. As one who has talked with him often in recent years, I can attest to the fact that he remains engagingly argumentative, somewhat bull-headed in a lighthearted way, wholeheartedly committed to the future of the New York Yankees and Major League Baseball, and fun to engage in conversation about his likes and dislikes. To me, George M. Steinbrenner, now age

77, is an original — a Yankee Doodle Dandy born on the fourth of July. Above all, he never flinched and did things his way. He is, like most of us, older and wiser about many things, and he richly deserves a plaque at Cooperstown.

an American
Original

Larry Doby was slow to anger, but that belied the depth of his resolve. As the first African American to play in the Major League Baseball's American League, he suffered the same indignities that Jackie Robinson did in the National League.

Robinson, the second baseman for the old Brooklyn Dodgers, beat Doby to the big leagues by less than three months, receiving considerably more media attention and national support. Some old-timers believe the blinding focus on Robinson delayed Larry Doby's entry into the Hall of Fame. The Veterans Committee voted Doby, a seven-time All-Star with the Cleveland Indians, the ultimate baseball honor in 1998. It was long overdue.

Renowned stars of the game, such as Ted Williams of the Boston Red Sox and Yogi Berra of the New York Yankees, were members of the committee that picked Doby. In conversation with me, Williams was apologetic that it took so long to get Doby elected, believing he was the ultimate gentleman, a distinct credit to the game, and "one helluva a ball player."

Berra agreed, feeling that his friend and neighbor from Paterson, New Jersey; deserved a place of honor "right next to Jackie." Larry Doby was "one of the American League's best outfielders," Yogi told me at the induction ceremony in Cooperstown. Williams and Berra went out of their way to underscore the greatness of Doby on and off the playing field.

Doby and Hall of Fame pitcher Bob Gibson of the St. Louis Cardinals were two of my on-field assistants at the American

Major League Baseball Photo

The American League's
First African American

Pioneer Larry Doby of the World Series champion Cleveland Indians.

League office in New York. Both had strong views on matters of substance and no reluctance to express those views. They rarely disagreed on baseball matters such as player discipline.

One day I made the mistake of telling Doby that I thought he had been disadvantaged by the disproportionate amount of attention that had been paid to the entry of Jackie Robinson. He was quick to respond that "Mr. Robinson" was the first, and deserving of the universal acclaim he had received. He refused to detract in any way from his National League counterpart, and he especially admired the way Jackie spoke out on controversial social issues later in his life. His wife Helen, an enormous source of strength for Doby through the years, felt the same way.

Doby and Robinson were not close friends, but each had respect for the other and each understood what the other had suffered. Larry Doby, Jr., once said that his father and Robinson had a genuine respect forged out of "pain, pride, and purpose."

Those who saw both of them play thought Robinson "played mad" and acted as though he had something to prove, while Doby was seen as a laid-back guy who was totally focused on being successful in the big leagues. Doby told me that he and Robinson had "the same goals" — winning and opening the doors of opportunity for other deserving minority athletes. Pitching great Joe Black, a teammate of Jackie Robinson in Brooklyn, told me Larry Doby was a "gentle soul" who wanted nothing taken away from Robinson. Teammate Bob Lemon of the Cleveland Indians said that in case of war he would want Doby in his foxhole.

Some baseball historians believe Doby's entry in 1947 took some pressure off Robinson, though both continued to be vilified around the country and were the recipients of unending hate mail. More than a few in the press thought Doby had the more difficult assignment because the American League was slower to integrate. Famed Bill Veeck and his son Mike, a highly successful minor league baseball team owner in Charleston, South Carolina, believed this to be true.

When Cleveland Indians owner Bill Veeck purchased Doby's contract for $10,000 from the Newark Eagles of the Negro National League, he told the 23-year-old black man that he was about to become a part of history. All Doby wanted was to play baseball and make enough to support a family. At the time he was leading the Negro National League with a gaudy batting average of .458.

In truth, Veeck and Doby had no idea how tough it would be with hordes of unruly fans hurling stinging insults and obscenities at both of them. Both learned early on to mask their true feelings, always taking the high road.

Doby struggled during his rookie season (1947), getting only five hits in 32 at-bats. He was determined to improve, and improve he did, leading the Indians to the American League pennant and the World Series championship in 1948. He was established, but he still felt compelled to work at a post office during the off-season, to make ends meet.

Many fans did not realize just how good Larry Doby really was as a ball player. He could hit the baseball "a country mile," Bob Lemon, a Hall of Fame pitcher, remembered. Larry was a .283 career hitter in 1,533 games, with 253 home runs and 970 runs batted. His achievements during a 13-year career were remarkable:

- seven-time All Star centerfielder;
- star of the 1948 World Series Champions, the Cleveland Indians;
- first black player to hit a home run in the World Series;
- first player to win championships in both the Negro Leagues and the Majors;

- first black player to win a home run title in Major League Baseball; and
- first black player to win a runs-batted-in title in the American League

Doby batted left-handed and threw right-handed. Bill Veeck thought he was art in motion, something rare to behold, and a human being and a ball player who was a model for all. Bill and his wife, Mary Frances, regarded the Doby family as part of their own.

Like Jackie Robinson, Doby was an all-around skilled athlete. Born in Camden, South Carolina, he moved at age eight with his mother to Paterson, New Jersey. There he was a standout in four sports at East Side High School, and he briefly attended Long Island University on a basketball scholarship.

He felt an obligation to enlist in the Navy. His Cleveland teammate Bob Feller, also a sailor, later said that Doby believed in his country and played the game the way it was meant to be played—hard and fair. Feller preceded Doby into the Hall of Fame and attended and applauded Doby's induction. He called the day "long overdue."

As one of my associates who advised on disciplinary matters, Larry laughed when telling me about an incident in 1957 when he was knocked to the ground by a high inside pitch from a New York Yankees pitcher. He charged the mound at old Comiskey Park and landed a punch to the pitcher's jaw.

The benches cleared, as they often do, and Doby suddenly had a sense of acceptance by his teammates who were ready to fight for him. He felt appreciated, but he later regretted throwing the punch. He was a member of the Chicago White Sox at the time of the incident. In contrast with Robinson, Doby refrained from on-field controversy in Cleveland, fearing it would hurt the reputation of other African Americans.

He also played the outfield for the Detroit Tigers late in his exceptional career.

In 1962, after his playing days were over in the American League, he joined former Dodger pitching ace Don Newcombe in integrating professional baseball in Japan. He returned to Chicago in 1978 to become the second African American to manage in the major leagues, working again for his ever-flamboyant Hall of Fame owner and friend Bill Veeck. The first African American to manage in the majors was Frank Robinson, a sensational power hitter with the Cincinnati Reds and the Baltimore Orioles.

Len Coleman, the former National League president, has vivid memories of Doby as a parent. He used to visit the Doby children in their Montclair home, and he remembers Larry being a stern and protective parent, but not in any way unfriendly. Coleman thought Doby could have been either a minister or teacher.

With that in mind, Coleman, the first African American to score a touchdown at Princeton University, was emotional when his alma mater honored Doby with an honorary Doctor of Humanities degree during its 150th commencement ceremony in June 1997. Faculty members at the Ivy League school hailed the recognition of Doby, believing that it was a credit to the school and to all mankind.

During one of many conversations in my office, Doby said "compassion and goodness are not determined by the color of one's skin." He recalled that some of his own teammates in Cleveland shunned him and refused to even play catch when he came to the majors, but not Ted Williams of the rival Boston Red Sox. Williams "reached out to me as a fellow human being. That gentleman stood tall in many ways; he was more than a great baseball player to me. He was a hero." Ted always sought Larry out before games to show solidarity.

Doby saw Williams as a person of courage, pointing out that he flew fighters in World War II and Korea, cutting into his prime as a player. The Red Sox star left fielder often referred to the Marines as his all-time favorite team; Boston was second. No one ever questioned his patriotism or his extraordinary abilities as a combat pilot and baseball hitter.

Larry Doby died on June 18, 2003, at age 79. His funeral at Montclair, New Jersey, drew an overflow crowd of baseball people and was a celebration of life, calling attention to how far mankind had traveled in understanding and respecting minorities and their accomplishments. President George W. Bush sent a message acknowledging the profound influence of Doby on the life of millions of Americans, and the commissioner of baseball called Doby a force for good everywhere. Many former players lowered their heads in thought and prayer.

Several months after Larry joined the American League staff, I told him about a brash kid from a small Nebraska town who read that Bill Veeck had hired a midget (Eddie Gaedel, August 19, 1951) to play for his old St. Louis Browns. The youngster wrote Veeck, asking for an immediate tryout. Known for his soft spot for children, the owner told the kid in a letter that he was a little too young, but he promised him a tryout after high school graduation. "That kid was me," I told Larry, and he smiled knowingly and said that Veeck had told him the story long ago. "That's when I knew we would get along," Doby said, and he was so right.

Interestingly, Gaedel gained immortality in the second game of a doubleheader against the Detroit Tigers in St. Louis when the three-foot, seven-inch player entered as a pinch hitter and drew a walk. The crowd roared with laughter and the other owners in Major League Baseball fumed with disgust. Veeck, a maverick showman, often taunted his colleagues, believing them to be preoccupied with their own importance. Veeck thought fun was good.

While coaching the New Jersey Nets, Larry Brown, long an admirer of Doby, arranged for Doby to have a job with the National Basketball Association team in New Jersey. Brown, who grew up in Brooklyn and was a regular at Ebetts Field as a youngster, frequently talked with Larry about baseball and his long-standing love for the game. Doby reminisced with him about the tough times when he and Jackie Robinson faced seemingly insurmountable odds.

"Everything about Larry Doby was good," Brown told me when he later coached the University of Kansas to a national basketball championship in 1988. The sports world echoes, without dissent, the coach's concluding thought.

Perhaps the
Greatest

Legendary football coach Tom Osborne and I contributed to each other's success. We once competed for the assistant to the chancellor position at the University of Nebraska-Lincoln in the late 1960s, and we both won. Tom decided to stay with coaching and I got the job.

He went on to win three national football championships while I later headed three large state universities (Illinois State University, West Virginia University, and the University of Kansas).

Chancellor Clifford M. Hardin told me at the time of my UNL appointment that "the perfect answer for me would have been to hire both of you." Tom, an assistant professor in educational psychology and measurement, and I once taught a course together in the Teachers College.

Osborne said that I was "ideally suited for the assistant position" because of my background as chief of staff for a governor of Nebraska, Frank B. Morrison. That might have been true, but he was without question the prohibitive favorite. Tom also said he wanted a chance to become Nebraska's head football coach, citing his love for the game, the university, and the state of Nebraska.

He realized that he was learning from one of America's premier coaches, Bob Devaney. Coach Devaney was an extrovert; Tom was almost shy, speaking only when spoken to and then responding with few words. They complemented each other. Devaney was elected to the College Football Hall of Fame after winning two national championships, and during his final season he elevated

Perhaps the Greatest

Football legend Tom Osborne (right)
and his Nebraska predecessor, Bob Devaney.

Osborne to the position of assistant head coach.

Devaney clearly wanted Osborne to be his replacement, even though several members of the Board of Regents and a few high rollers from Omaha and Lincoln were apprehensive. Many people wanted Devaney to continue coaching and not become athletic director, which they thought would be a waste of his considerable on-field talents. "Anyone can be an athletic director," one contributor wrote the Board of Regents.

Along with my administrative colleagues, I lobbied for Osborne to become head football coach once I knew that was Devaney's best judgment and recommendation. One of my assignments at UNL was to work with the Regents, who clearly loved Devaney, hung on his every word, and respected Osborne. Devaney pretty much closed the deal when he announced that Osborne, as an assistant, had been the principal architect of the offensive plan that resulted in his two national championships.

The case for Osborne was compelling, or so it seemed, and the Regents finally relented and went along, as did most of the boisterous Nebraska fans and influential sports columnists across the state. Osborne remained a mystery to many.

Dr. Tom Osborne is arguably the finest college coach who ever patrolled the sidelines of a football field. In his quarter of a century as a head coach, he posted 255 wins, 49 losses, and 3 ties—the best record among Division 1-A coaches at the time. His record was one of extraordinary consistency. Devaney delighted in the success of his protégé and fiercely defended him when there was even a hint of public criticism.

Coach Osborne never won fewer than nine games in a season during his illustrious career. His winning percentage was 83.6. During his last five seasons, the Cornhuskers won 60 games and lost only three, and they collected three national championship trophies. Osborne, the master of understatement, once said, "Those were pretty good years for Nebraska, I guess."

Osborne was a public figure and a private person, one that players respected and fellow head coaches revered. Fans never really knew or understood him, only his wins. He was most at home when he was wearing a headset at Memorial Stadium in Lincoln, talking to assistants in the press box, and calling offensive plays. He rarely changed expressions in public view, and always assumed responsibility for a failed play. He was stoic after an infrequent loss.

After numerous conversations about Tom Osborne, I have concluded that many of the people who worked with or played for him never really knew him. He seemed to live within a competitiveness zone, a place that left little room for anything but football, winning, family, and love for his university and state. He seemed to discourage small talk, but he was never impolite.

He always supported his players, even when the national media questioned his motives. Unfortunate off-field behavior was addressed behind closed doors at Nebraska and he refused to cast aspersions in public. "Tom was guided by conscience, not by what a bunch of sports writers thought at the time," Devaney once told me. Reporters, primarily from national publications, accused Osborne of refusing to properly discipline players in order to keep them eligible and on the field, thus enhancing the chances of winning.

Some columnists from the East even questioned his election to the College Football Hall of Fame, which spurred widespread support from his coaching contemporaries around the country. His former players were riled and vocal, to say the least. Those reporters who thought Osborne would try to win "at any cost" simply did not know the man. That philosophy was inconsistent with who he was and how he thought and lived.

Major financial contributors were often annoyed when Osborne would say "winning is not as important as playing the game right and playing up to our potential." They were fixated on winning conference and national championships. Osborne was Big 8 Conference coach of the year in 1975, 76, 80, 88, 92, 93, and 94, and the conference was widely regarded as one of the strongest in America.

During his remarkable career, he led the Huskers to 25 bowl games, 13 conference titles, and three national championships. Without question, he and Bob Devaney spoiled Nebraskans with continual success and national rankings. Fans were conditioned to win, and with regularity.

Warren Buffett of Omaha, the world's second richest person, is a long-time friend of Osborne and believes in his unquestioned integrity and the way he coached the game. Buffett once had the annual report of Berkshire Hathaway printed in red and white to honor Osborne and recognize the school colors. Buffett is a UNL graduate.

Buffett was among the first to contribute to Osborne's successful 2000 campaign for a seat in the U.S. House of Representatives. He was elected as a republican three times from Nebraska's sprawling 3rd congressional district. He won high marks as a representative who studied the issues and voted his conscience. He missed only 84 of 3,423 votes in his six years in Congress. Osborne became popular as a speaker for GOP congressional candidates across the country.

He made an unsuccessful run for governor in the 2006 gubernatorial primary.

Osborne grew up in Hastings, Nebraska, where he was all-state in football and basketball and was the state's High School Athlete of the Year in 1955. He was widely recruited, but stayed at home and attended Hastings College where his father and grandfather had gone. His loyalty was apparent to many in his hometown.

Osborne quarterbacked the Hastings College football team and went on to become Nebraska's College Athlete of the Year in 1959. He then played professional football for three years with Washington and San Francisco.

He joined the coaching staff of Bob Devaney at the University of Nebraska-Lincoln in 1962, serving as a graduate assistant, receiver's coach, and finally as offensive coordinator. "His potential was clear from the start," said Don Bryant, former sports editor of The Lincoln Star and long-time sports information director and associate athletic director. "He was a person of intellect and offensive creativity, and Coach Devaney appreciated that fact."

Osborne was never a run of the mill football coach at UNL. While serving as a graduate assistant, he earned master's and doctoral degrees in educational psychology. He burned a lot of midnight oil in the early days, and without fanfare, wanting to be a role model for student athletes and in a position to teach someday.

Osborne took enormous pride in the fact that he had recruited and coached a record 46 Academic All-Americans at UNL and had a graduation rate of 84 percent among his players, one of the highest percentages in the country at the time. He was especially sensitive to the educational needs of African American athletes and he helped to establish model academic support programs that were adopted by many other colleges and universities.

It is interesting that some of his finest players at Nebraska were not recruited by other schools. Osborne and Devaney believed in the importance of a walk-on program, giving determined youngsters, especially from smaller communities, a chance to play on the big stage. The ultimate reward for these players was membership on the varsity football team, becoming someone who others in the community regarded as a Husker hero, and, of course, obtaining a prized and often needed scholarship.

Nebraska's perennial challenger for Big 8 Conference supremacy during the Osborne years was the Sooners of the University of Oklahoma. Head coaches Barry Switzer and Tom Osborne had an annual battle of wits, often introducing new and sometimes trick plays, usually before a national television audience. Fans from the two schools thought the coaches were antagonistic toward each other and that added to the drama of the game. The members of the press corps thrived on the rivalry between the coaches and their programs.

Truth be known, Switzer and Osborne liked each other, and thrived on the high-visibility competition. Switzer was brash; Osborne was reserved. Switzer was a risk taker; Osborne was an organized planner. But coaches Switzer and Osborne were masterful in bringing out the best in their players and growing national interest in the college game.

When Osborne turned to politics, Switzer came to Lincoln to campaign for him. He called Osborne a person who brought credit to the often stained world of politics. Their long-term bond was obvious to all who saw them. They were, and remain, good friends who occasionally enjoy talking about the old days.

Jeff Kinney, the All-American halfback on the national championship teams of 1970 and 71, provided interesting insight on Coach Osborne during a trip to our hometown—McCook, Nebraska—where we served as parade marshals for Heritage Days 2007. He remembers the stark differences between coaches Osborne and Devaney.

Osborne recruited Kinney and made trips to southwest Nebraska, offering little more than an expression that he and

Coach Devaney thought Jeff could be an important member of the Huskers. That was all Jeff Kinney needed to commit to UNL. Kinney found Osborne to be honest and to the point, and they once went fishing but the conversation was limited as was the number of fish.

Devaney made people laugh, while Osborne made people think, Kinney thought, and together they made the football players better competitors and people. Values were to be understood and respected at UNL. Both coaches were expert in their use of Xs and Os.

Osborne and his wife Nancy always took time to give back to society, forming a foundation that is designed to foster youth education. They regularly taught Sunday school at a Methodist Church in Lincoln.

I believe Tom Osborne's compass is stuck in the right direction. Perhaps it always has been. Never willing to turn his back on his university or his state, the 70-year-old icon agreed to return to serve as interim athletic director in 2007. Chancellor Harvey Perlman singled him out to right the ship and return the Huskers to national prominence.

Cheers have returned to state of Nebraska, a place in the Midlands where corn, wheat, cattle, and winning football are central ingredients to life.

a Winning
Choice

A day before Roy Williams was to be announced as the new men's basketball coach at the University of Kansas, three of the school's largest financial contributors asked to meet with me. They were in no mood for pleasantries on that July morning in 1988.

They were single-minded in telling me that, as chancellor of their university, I had an inescapable obligation to hire an established basketball coach with a winning record, not an unknown assistant from the University of North Carolina at Chapel Hill.

They reminded me that the preceeding season's Jayhawks were NCAA national champions, and a wrong-headed appointment would threaten the success of KU's most cherished sport and the school's recently launched fundraising drive. They also said a mistake would raise a dark cloud over my years as chancellor.

My reasoned responses were met with silence and steely stares that day.

The athletic director, Dr. Bob Frederick, believed in Roy Williams and felt he would bring enormous upside to the historic program, which was then, in terms of victories, one of the three most successful college basketball programs in the country. Bob was a person of unquestioned integrity and sound judgment and I was fortunate to have him at my side.

Bob and I stood our ground, believing Dean Smith, a Kansas native and Hall of Fame coach at North Carolina, when he said he would stake his professional reputation on Roy Williams and

University of North Carolina at Chapel Hill Photo

A National Champion

Tar Heel Basketball Coach Roy Williams.

his chances for success at his alma mater. Smith also had recommended former Tar Heel Larry Brown five years earlier, and Brown coached the Jayhawks to a national championship. What he said made sense, if we were willing to suffer for a while.

Roy Williams was not a popular choice at the outset, but he moved immediately to convince many of the most vocal critics of his skills as a basketball person. In his first season, he coached an undermanned Kansas team to 19 wins; fans were surprised and upbeat. His potential was clearly obvious.

Williams was seen by other coaches around the country as a promising and someday formidable competitor who ran a North Carolina-like program. He regularly engaged students and fans in open forums, hearing them out on ways to strengthen the perception of Jayhawk basketball, on ways to engender understanding and needed support.

Williams responded with clarity to all written and oral inquires, some of them profane, and he usually incorporated a humorous story or two. He was skilled at being self-effacing and believable at the same time. Faculty members embraced his openness and charm and his commitment to the student athlete; they wanted to be helpful to him and his assistant coaches through innovative tutoring programs. Faculty members quickly bought into the Williams program and its objectives, and they devoted countless hours to the committed student athletes.

Several senior faculty members from governance even thought Williams would be an excellent classroom teacher. In less than a year, Williams was treated as a trustworthy peer by even the most difficult professors. In contrast, Larry Brown had never courted faculty and was uneasy around some of the more critical ones who insisted that collegiate sports were over-emphasized and out of control. Brown was fundamentally shy when he was off the basketball court.

Even traditional rivalries with the Universities of Missouri and Oklahoma were played with unusual civility because their veteran coaches liked the first-year coach at KU and his articulated values. Williams was humble, but strong in his convictions. It was difficult for Coach Williams to recruit in 1988 because the Jayhawks were on probation for actions taken before his arrival. He never complained; he simply redoubled his efforts, especially in the rough-and-tumble world of athletics recruiting.

My once-surly alumni visitors soon forgot their reservations about Coach Williams and became great fans and supporters. The KU fundraising campaign they had feared for was a smashing success and exceeded all expectations. It was, in fact, the most successful drive in school history and in the Midwestern states.

Popular ESPN basketball commentator Dick Vitale was among the first to hop on the Roy Williams bandwagon, saying the hire was "truly sensational" for the University of Kansas. He often referred to Frederick and Williams on television as "the ideal team, baby." He believed that, with them in place and with continued support from the university administration, the Kansas program would be a perennial winner. And he was right.

Vitale saw Williams building a foundation, much like the one constructed at North Carolina. He especially liked the new coach's work ethic and the unique way he recruited a prospective player and his parents. He was a Dean Smith in the making, Vitale thought.

One thing that played well for Coach Williams in Kansas was the fact that at North Carolina he had recruited Michael Jordan, regarded by many as the best athlete ever to play college and professional basketball. Jordan came to Lawrence to help Williams with his summer basketball camps, which drew huge numbers of youngsters from across the state and the region. Without question, the Jordan presence did much to enhance the image of Williams as a winner and of basketball at KU. Most die-hard fans were convinced that Williams would attract another Jordan, this time for the Crimson and Blue.

Roy Williams surpassed all reasonable expectations at Kansas. His 15-year record with the Jayhawks was breathtaking, almost unbelievable to studied observers of the game. From 1988 to 2003, he won 418 games, second in wins only to legendary Phog Allen, who had recruited consensus All-Americans Clyde Lovellete and Wilt Chamberlin to the storied program on the Plains. Williams became a trusted father figure to his players, always willing to sit down and work through their personal and collegiate problems. His graduation rates were consistently among the highest when compared to other winning programs.

When Roy Williams announced that he was returning to North Carolina, his alma mater, in 2003, there were heartfelt tears throughout Kansas and loud cheers across the wooded campus at Chapel Hill. A bomb had landed. Many in Kansas were stunned, briefly without direction, and bitter, but most of them came to realize just how much Roy Williams had meant to KU and the reputation of the basketball program. He built and left a winner.

The Lawrence, Kansas, Journal-World wrote, "Williams is a winner, not only on the basketball court but also as a person. Collegiate sports need more coaches such as Williams, men and women who set an example for others to try and match."

In his years as a high-profile head coach, Williams has won national coach of the year honors six times. Amazingly, after eight years of coaching, he had won more basketball games than any coach of equal tenure. The same could be said after each season, nine through 19. Furthermore, he is the only coach to win a game in 18 consecutive NCAA tournaments and is third all-time in tournament games behind his mentor Dean Smith, and Lute Olson, who coached at the Universities of Iowa and Arizona.

Williams began his 20th season with a career mark of 524 wins and 131 losses, averaging more than 27 wins a season. His winning percentage of 80 percent was the best among active coaches with at least ten seasons as a head coach, and he now stands behind only Clair Bee, Adolph Rupp, and John Wooden in history. His 2007-08 Tar Heels were ranked first in preseason polls.

The Asheville, North Carolina, native with the down-home manner has won more games than any coach in the country in the past six seasons. When his North Carolina players won the 2005 national championship, they played disciplined and unselfish basketball, familiar traits he instilled during his days in Allen Field House at Lawrence.

In four seasons at Chapel Hill, Williams has led the Tar Heels to a 106 wins and 30 losses record and two NCAA number one seeds.

Dean Smith likens Williams to Tiger Woods in golf: "They have the whole package." In conversation with me, Smith said that the 1972 Carolina graduate is very bright, knows basketball like few others do, can quickly judge talent, is an excellent and patient coach at practice, makes good game-time decisions, and is highly organized.

Roy Williams is what you see: pleasant, open, accessible, and highly competitive. He has friends everywhere he has been and he loves people and especially college students. He gets dead serious, however, when it comes to coaching basketball; laughs are few on the court.

I believe the most compelling reason for his many successes was on display at the 2007 Naismith Memorial Basketball Hall of Fame induction ceremony in Springfield, Massachussetts. Twenty-five of the finest college basketball players of the past 25 years from both Kansas and North Carolina were there as members of the extended Williams family.

It was the largest turnout of players in the history of an induction at the Hall. Standouts such as Paul Pierce, Sean May, Jacque Vaughn, Raymond Fenton, Raef LaFrentz, Marvin Williams, and Kirk Hinrich were in attendance as "Roy's boys," not as either Jayhawks or Tar Heels.

Sixteen of his players have been selected in the first round of the National Basketball Association draft. Coach Dean Smith and coach Larry Brown, another Hall of Fame coach with ties to Lawrence and Chapel Hill, shared the podium at the ceremony with the newest inductee, Roy Williams. Larry Brown, by the way, was hailed as one of the college game's premier bench coaches, a proven genius who never felt comfortable recruiting young people and left much of that to assistant coaches.

Importantly, Williams likes the people he recruits and he likes their parents. He wants them to know that they are becoming part of a new family for life. He entertains them in his home and his wife, Wanda, prepares a home-cooked meal. Roy and Wanda Williams have two children, Scott and Kimberly, and they thoroughly enjoy college basketball.

Williams carefully learns what makes a recruit tick by listening first and talking second. He pays special attention to parents and their questions and concerns about college life. He wants them to be comfortable with his objectives, supportive of his ways, and informed about the program and its rigorous requirements.

Williams sounds like a dedicated teacher when he speaks of the importance of a college education. He wants his players to graduate and be prepared for life after basketball. He takes a lot of time for questions and he answers with candor and ease.

Michael Jordan remembers Williams as a person "you could sit down and talk to; he wasn't intimidating," and famed All-American guard Jerry West of West Virginia believes a Williams-coached team "plays the right way." When West was general manager of the Los Angeles Lakers, he approached Roy about the head coaching position. I believe, however, that Williams is best suited for the campus, not the National Basketball Association.

The coach startled many at the Hall of Fame ceremony when he apologized to Jayhawk players from the mid-1990s for not leading them to a Final Four, despite winning some 33 games a year from 1996-98. "That tells you the type of person he is," said Paul Pierce, a KU All-American and NBA all-star with the Boston Celtics. Another All-American and 10-year NBA veteran, Raef LaFrentz, added, "He didn't fail me; he aided me."

Williams was quick to point out that his induction would motivate him to do even better, making the people who selected him feel they made the right choice. He believes that "outstanding recruits can make a coach look brighter than he really is." One can assume that Coach Williams will be racking up even more frequent flier miles, since he rarely delegates during the recruiting season. Williams believes that some coaching responsibilities can be delegated, but not recruiting.

Witnessing the induction of his former basketball coach was an emotional experience for Bob Frederick, now a professor in the School of Education at the University of Kansas. In Williams, he realized a dream of what greatness is and what it should be. That day Frederick had a right to pause, shed a tear, and take enormous pride in the extraordinary contributions of Roy Williams to intercollegiate athletics in the United States.

a **Meteor**
for the Ages

Gale Sayers was simply the very best at what he did. For nine football seasons in college and the professional ranks, he ran with mesmerizing grace, blinding speed, previously unseen moves, and unquestioned courage. He was the real deal.

He was painfully shy. Some thought he was arrogant and unapproachable, but nothing could have been further from the truth. He grew up poor and in a ghetto. His interests were pretty much limited to football and track at Omaha Central High School and to music. Books were for the other students.

Gale once claimed he left high school "without learning a thing," and college had little appeal for him. He considered joining the Army. After his senior year of football, he got more than 100 offers from major universities such as Notre Dame, Northwestern, Minnesota, Nebraska, and Kansas. He was more interested in taking the recruiting trips than going to college.

His family often did not have enough money for food. His father, Roger, worked for $65 a week polishing cars and he had to pay $75 for rent. His mother, Bernice, did her best to make ends meet, preparing a variety of meals with chicken feet.

His older brother Roger was a promising student and a track standout, winning Nebraska Class A high school titles in the 100- and 220-yard dashes. He went on to the Municipal University of Omaha to excel on the cinders and in the classroom, and he made the U. S. track team that competed against Russia. He beat

University of Kansas Archives Photo

A Meteor for the Ages

Gale Sayers, consensus All-American at Kansas
and Chicago Bears All-Pro halfback.

former world record holder Bob Hayes in the 100-yard dash in 1962. Gale's younger brother Ronnie went to Omaha University and played football.

Gale ran track in high school as well, winning gold medals in the low hurdles, the 880 relay, and the broad jump. He led Omaha Central to the city title in football and the state championship in track. He also made the All-America high school football team which put him on everyone's radar screen.

As a football player, Gale freely admitted that "nothing ever worried me," and he had an injury-free high school career. He thought with his feet and he never ran a football with fear as a companion. He was unpretentious with his boyhood friends who were largely African American.

He especially enjoyed his trip to Notre Dame, but decided against the legendary football program because it was too far from home. He liked the coaches and the campus but thought he should go to the University of Nebraska because it was only 60 miles from Omaha. This way he could keep in touch with his high school friends.

Nebraska put considerable pressure on Gale and his parents, who favored the Lincoln site. His campus visit was a disaster, as one of the NU halfbacks wanted to jump him because he wore a letter sweater from high school, one that had decorations for making All-State in football and gold medals for track.

Gale remembers that the University of Nebraska relegated him and an African American from Omaha Central to a dormitory basement where the heating pipes ran along the ceiling and kept banging all night. Several high school recruits from Oklahoma were assigned nicer rooms upstairs. What troubled Gale most was learning that Nebraska had 44 African American athletes and only two African American female students. Bill Jennings, then head football coach at NU and a decent human being, came to Omaha and apologized to Gale for the unfortunate turn of events.

Meanwhile, the University of Kansas had young Sayers in its sights, and flamboyant head coach Jack Mitchell sent his best recruiter to Omaha to persuade Gale to visit Lawrence. He agreed, and instantly liked the beauty of the sprawling campus that occupied the top of a hill. He liked the fact that it was a good school for the African American athlete and that Wilt Chamberlain played basketball on Mount Oread. Sayers also liked Mitchell and his plans for him.

The gifted halfback/kick receiver made a second visit to the campus, being impressed with the university's reputation, especially in the Omaha area, and the fact it had a winning football team in need of additional offensive strength. He decided to cast his lot with the Jayhawks, believing he could make it in college as an athlete and a student. He was accompanied by his high school girlfriend, Linda. His only regret, and it was a painful one, was that several of his best friends did not have the grades to get into Kansas.

Nebraska football fans were unforgiving when one of their own greats decided in favor of another state. Sports columns, especially in Omaha and Lincoln, were brimming with venom that would not go away anytime soon. Many thought Coach Jennings was fired because of Gale's controversial decision. Jennings thought so too. His replacement was colorful Bob Devaney who came from the University of Wyoming and won Big 8 Conference championships for the Huskers in two of the next three years, largely with the recruits of Jennings.

Mike Shinn, a promising African American tight end from Topeka, Kansas, was Gale's first roommate. He was big and strong and would eventually become an All Big 8 Conference player and a graduate with a degree in engineering. He had a successful career with General Electric and was elected by his peers to the Board of Directors of the KU Alumni Association. Shinn quickly saw the potential of his new friend as a player and a human being. He encouraged Sayers. Sayers believed in God and offered nightly prayers in his dormitory room. He and Shinn learned from each other's strengths and weaknesses and they formed a bond at KU that would last a lifetime.

What Shinn saw up close was one of the century's premier athletes and a person with some fundamental insecurities. Sayers transformed himself when he ran onto a football field, entering a world of blissful challenge. He loved every facet of the game, and he treated it with respect.

During my 13 years as chancellor of the University of Kansas, I talked with Coach Mitchell on a number of occasions about "Sayer," as he called him. The adjectives flowed freely when he recalled Sayers being so fleet you "didn't have time to cheer his touchdowns."

The Sayers legend started taking form when the freshmen at KU were allowed to play only two football games. In his first game against Kansas State, he electrified the crowd and sports reporters with a 51-yard touchdown run. Those from the media were amazed by his speed, agility, and grace, reporting that they had never seen anyone quite like him.

The press in Kansas City took special interest in Sayers and his next game against the University of Missouri and their top recruit, freshman running back Johnny Roland. They billed the game as a duel between two of America's finest young runners. Interestingly, the game ended in a 21-21 tie, but Gale amassed 161 yards on 20 carries and Roland gained 87 yards on 19 tries. The "Kansas Comet," as the media began to call Sayers, scored against

Missouri on runs of 25, 1, and 79 yards. Gale scored all six of the Jayhawk freshman team touchdowns.

Anticipation ran high among Kansas football fans as Gale moved to varsity status. If you were a Jayhawk, the thought of number 48 streaking down the sidelines en route to another touchdown was something to build dreams. Opposing coaches and their aides were at work devising ways to slow Sayers, but few would be successful.

There was something far more threatening to Sayers than any defensive line from Nebraska or Oklahoma—he was not making it in the classroom. He failed English and had a batch of Ds, resulting in academic probation. He had to attend summer school to be eligible for football in the fall. He was dispirited, but the press never picked up on the academic problem.

Sayers returned to Omaha in June and asked Linda to marry him. She said yes and they were off to Lawrence with a U-Haul the morning after the wedding. He told his friends that marriage helped settle him down and his grades improved dramatically. Linda provided encouragement, stability, and discipline.

Like most young couples, they struggled financially. Athletic scholarships were not generous in those days and Linda went to work on an assembly line at the Hallmark card factory in Lawrence. In the off-season Gale took odd jobs, such as one in the press room of the Lawrence Journal-World. Publisher Dolph Simons, Jr., remembered Sayers coming and going on a bicycle. "He worked hard and people liked him," Simons recalled.

The stars were aligned for Gale Sayers as he entered his sophomore year at the University of Kansas. The media in the Midwest touted him as one of the finest running backs in the rugged Big 8 Conference, a league that included some of the country's finest football teams and players. Sports reporters on the national scene took notice of Sayers and saw great things ahead for the swift Jayhawks runner. Some even mentioned the possibility of Sayers being an All America halfback.

Gale was at peace with himself, his new wife, and his surroundings. The newlyweds had an active social life, enjoying friends and the simplicity of their surroundings. They often made light about their financial struggles along with other young couples. Gale had a new resolve to learn and to be a good student, but there was a problem that he tried to shield from the outside world. He stuttered and shied away from the press as much as possible, and he was uneasy around large groups of students and fans.

One of Gale's early instructors was Tom Hedrick, who also did play-by-play for the Jayhawks Radio Network and the Kansas City Chiefs. He was troubled by Gale's inability to speak well or even make himself understood at times. Hedrick went to Coach Mitchell and asked for permission to work with Gale on improving his speech patterns; Mitchell said yes. Gale remembers his first speech in class as being "one of the worst experiences in my life." He and Hedrick set out on a rigorous path that would eventually make Gale more comfortable with himself. The first semester speech class was a success for both the student and the instructor, but considerably more work was in the offing.

Tom Hedrick and Jack Mitchell realized that Sayers was likely to be a big star—one that would leave the sports world in awe of his on-field exploits. It was imperative, they thought, for him to be able to express himself in a public setting before a crowd of people. This would mean confidence, opportunity, and riches for the young man from a ghetto on Omaha's north side.

Another person who assisted Sayers was Jesse Milan. He helped Sayers with his speech and study habits. Milan had been working with African American athletes and students at KU for a number of years. Sayers first met him on a recruiting trip to Lawrence. He sought out the lonesome young student athlete when he enrolled and they became friends. Sayers has recalled that his proudest achievement at KU was not making All America teams or setting a Big 8 career rushing record, but rather making a three-point grade average before his senior year.

Even with a marginal supporting cast for his three years of varsity football, Sayers was a certifiable star on the national scene and a genuine cult figure in the state of Kansas and the entire Midwest. He was a two-time All American, featured often in national magazines and on the football clips shown in movie theatres across America. His face became synonymous with big-time college football; he was recognized everywhere. He remained humble, always humble, letting his gaudy statistics at KU speak for him.

At the University of Kansas he experienced a very productive three-year varsity career in the early 1960s. He established Big 8 records by rushing for 2,675 yards, catching passes for 408 yards, and adding 835 yards on kick returns. He led the Jayhawks in touchdowns, rushing, and kickoff returns during his remarkable career.

Perhaps his most memorable run in college came in 1963 against the highly regarded University of Nebraska Cornhuskers in Lincoln. I remember thinking that day that Gale Sayers could actually glide and change directions at will as he winged his way to a 99-yard touchdown. The field at Memorial Stadium was littered with defenders in red jerseys and the record crowd of 39,844 fans was without voice. The electrifying run still makes most college football highlight films and it was the longest run from scrimmage in the storied history of the Big 8. Hall of Fame coach Bob Devaney would later tell me when I was a professor at Nebraska that "Gale Sayers was from another planet. He was virtually impossible to defend." Another Hall of Fame coach, then NU assistant Tom Osborne, remembers the run as "one of the greatest ever seen."

Opposing coaches from the Big 8 questioned why Kansas so often used Gale as a decoy on offense. "I would have run him a lot more than Kansas did," Devaney said. Osborne would have too. Another legendary coach who saw Sayers up close was Bud Wilkinson of Oklahoma who said, "Sayers can fly when he's running at a 90-degree angle." Gale once ran for a 93-yard touchdown in a Kansas win over the Sooners.

Sayers remembers many things about his days as a college player, but one that stands out above the rest was his last football game in Lincoln when the Nebraska fans, with the clock running down late in the game, gave him a standing ovation. Admittedly, many Husker partisans never got over the disappointment of not getting Sayers in scarlet and cream colors, but they showed their unquestioned appreciation and respect for his stunning talent and proven courage. He left for the bus trip back to Lawrence with a lump in his throat.

In those days there were two professional football leagues and teams from both had a wanting eye on Gale Sayers and what he could mean for them. Sayers was personally recruited by Lamar Hunt, the long-time owner of the Kansas City Chiefs of the American Football League, and the Chiefs pledged to make the former Kansas halfback their number-one choice, certain that he was going to rewrite the record books. Affable Buddy Young contacted Sayers on behalf of the National Football League and the commissioner's spokesman made a persuasive case for the NFL, stressing the superiority of the pension plan over the one offered by the AFL.

He also emphasized the difference in prestige between the

leagues, and the importance of "markets." Young did not mention the NFL teams that were interested in Sayers until the last minute. The Giants, the Bears, and San Francisco were looking at him, and Young was quick to point out that all were big market teams. Sayers thought New York would be okay, Linda preferred San Francisco, and neither knew much about Chicago. But the Bears made him a number-one draft selection along with the powerful Dick Butkus from the University of Illinois.

At the urging of Young, who was from the Windy City and who would become a close friend and adviser, Gale Sayers signed with the Bears for $25,000 a year for four seasons and a $50,000 bonus. Gale thought he had made the right decision, certain that he would be playing with and against the best athletes in professional football. He liked owner-coach George Halas from the start, and they would later bond in a father-son type relationship.

What happened after the signing was truly remarkable. In his first game, an exhibition against the Los Angeles Rams, Sayers sprinted 77 yards on a punt return, 93 yards on a kickoff, and passed for a 25-yard touchdown. The Chicago media could not get enough of the quiet, unassuming new star; his name was everywhere. In his inaugural season, Gale scored 22 touchdowns and 132 points, both then rookie records. He dashed for six touchdowns against the San Francisco 49ers and was an overwhelming choice for NFL Rookie of the Year in 1965.

It is hard to believe that Sayers played in only 68 professional football games with the Chicago Bears. His impact on the sport was so great that at age 34 he became the youngest player ever to be selected to the Professional Football Hall of Fame. He entered the Canton, Ohio, shrine in 1977 with Frank Gifford, Bart Starr, Forrest Gregg, and Bill Willis. Halas, by now a true mentor, introduced Sayers at the emotional induction ceremony, saying, "If you've never seen Gale play, his like will never be seen again."

The greatness of Gale Sayers should be not measured by statistics alone, according to John Hadl, another All American from the University of Kansas and a Pro Hall of Fame quarterback with the San Diego Chargers and the Los Angeles Rams. "Gale was a marked man from day one on every play he ran with the Bears. Defenses were especially designed to stop him, to get him off the field and out of the game. Few other players of his time had this threat or this challenge," Hadl explained. "Only Jim Brown had that much of a problem."

As a high school football player in Omaha, Sayers idolized Brown and was taken with his size, speed, quickness, and resolve. Like Brown, Sayers had great hands, making him an excellent receiver out of the backfield, and, like the Cleveland great, he returned kickoffs and occasionally threw passes.

When people talk about the storied Chicago Bears there are three names that always surface: Gale Sayers, Dick Butkus, and George Halas. Sayers and Butkus had an immediate and lasting impact on the NFL and the generations of players to follow. They joined Coach Halas in Chicago at the same time; both rejected offers from the Kansas City Chiefs and the AFL. Butkus lined up behind the ball on defense and Sayers spent his time on offense. They set a challenging standard for those who would follow.

What the Bears needed during their remarkable era were a couple more gifted athletes; with them Chicago would have been a consistent winner. Butkus and Sayers, always the best of friends, had their numbers retired by the Bears on the same night at Soldier Field in 1994. Sayers believes today that Halas had the "foresight and strength" to make the National Football League happen.

Perhaps Sayers' most rewarding recognition came in 1969 when he was picked as a first team running back on the NFL's All-

Time Millennium Team. There he was with his boyhood idol, Jim Brown. Sayers had just agreed to a new three-year contract that made him the highest paid player in the NFL, but his career would come to a premature end in 1970 when he suffered another serious knee injury, his second as a member of the Bears. He was 29 years old and he had few places to go. Some writers, such as Chuck Woodling of the Lawrence Journal-World, tied Sayers to Sandy Koufax who entered baseball's Hall of Fame after having only six exceptional years as a pitcher for the Los Angeles Dodgers.

Prior to his career-ending injury, Sayers had agreed to do a book focusing on his life in football, what it took for him to recover from his first and most serious knee injury, and how as an accomplished pro halfback he was trying to learn to "run again." He titled the book I Am Third, coming from a sign on his track coach's desk at the University of Kansas. Bill Easton explained, "The Lord is first, my friends are second, and I am third." That explanation became a part of the young athlete's mantra, values, thoughts, and actions. The book eventually had a profound impact on millions of men, women, and children, especially as they read the segment about Brian Piccolo's courageous battle with cancer, in an adaption for the popular Look Magazine and later in the movie adaptation, Brian's Song. It became the highest-rated television movie at the time and remains a late-night favorite to this day.

Sayers and Piccolo were the first integrated roommates on the Chicago Bears in 1969, a subject for much media fodder. They enjoyed the attention and had fun with it. Piccolo and Sayers were opposites, with one talking a lot and the other saying little. They became inseparable friends on and off the football field. Piccolo died in 1970, leaving Sayers with a profound sense of loss that he still feels today.

Linda and Gale were married in their teens, and with the passing of years, they discovered they had little in common. They divorced in 1971.

Sayers caught a break in 1973 when his alma mater, the University of Kansas, asked him to return as assistant director of athletics. He married Ardie Bullard, a mother with four sons from Omaha, in 1973. The return to KU gave him the chance to complete his bachelor's degree in physical education and to pursue and earn a master's in educational administration. No one was more popular or successful with alumni groups and big contributors than Gale Sayers, who grew to like raising money for athletics.

Due to his clear success as a fund raiser at KU and his favorable name recognition, Gale became athletics director at Southern Illinois University in Carbondale in 1976. He was the first African American athletics director at a major state university. He reminded prospective student athletes and their parents that life was short for a football player, but a college degree was forever. He lived what he said. I remember sitting in a driving rain storm with Sayers at Illinois State University watching my Redbirds play his Salukis. I was the president of ISU at the time and he was the drenched athletics director from SIU. I do not remember who won, but I was struck by the conviction in Sayers' voice when he talked about the need to graduate many more African American football players. Sayers knew the ghettos of Chicago and Omaha and he saw, first hand, what they could do to an undereducated young person of color.

Sayers yearned to return to the NFL as an administrator with one of the teams, but that was not to be. Instead, he returned to Chicago after his years at Southern Illinois and launched a business that became Sayers Computer Source, a premier minority-owned business. Since its founding, the company has grown to include four branches across the country with revenues of millions of dollars. Highly popular with minority businesses, Sayers Computer Source sells computers and offers operating systems, systems integration, and consulting services. In recognition of his sizeable success, Sayers was voted into the prestigious Chicago Area Entrepreneurship Hall of Fame. He was proud to be cited as more than an athlete.

Gale Sayers knows the people who make things happen in America's third largest city. He has worked for numerous charitable causes with prominent leaders like Jesse Jackson, Jerry Reinsdorf, Mayor Richard J. Daley and his son, Mayor Richard M. Daly. He is a favorite among business leaders. Sayers has devoted countless hours to deserving organizations like the Boys & Girls Club of America, Marklund Children's Home, the Boy Scouts of America, the American Cancer Society, the Better Boys Foundation, Junior Achievement, and the Cradle Adoption Agency. He is a popular speaker for charitable events in Chicago.

It was Reinsdorf, the successful owner of both the Chicago Bulls and the White Sox, who said, "Gale Sayers is more than a hero of the gridiron. He is a living symbol of one who has made a far reaching and lasting difference. He is an ideal gentlemen and citizen. He is one of us." In my eyes, Gale was one with "God-given talent" on the football field who refused to let life bring him to his knees. He was, and is, an inspiration to generations.

He played for glory long before all star halfbacks in professional football received multi-year contracts worth millions of dollars. He and Jim Brown were legends, to be sure—legends without the benefit of weighty portfolios. Yet Gale Sayers became well to do with the acquired skills of a modern-day business leader. After proving that he was an accomplished fundraiser for athletic programs at the University of Kansas and Southern Illinois University, he founded a successful business in Chicago. His business became a national model. Gale Sayers was more than a superb athlete; he was an inspiration to many young people who needed timely encouragement. Furthermore, he frequently shared his personal resources with deserving communities and national societal charities.

Living a
Dream

Jerry Reinsdorf voted to eliminate my job as president of Major League Baseball's American League in late 1999, joining his brethren in ownership in accepting a sweeping recommendation from Commissioner Bud Selig to consolidate all the substantive responsibilities of the two leagues under his direction. It was a historic game of hardball because the presidents of the American and National Leagues were in place long before there was a commissioner, and because the owners had just voted unanimously for three-year extensions for the presidents.

Selig argued that it was important to adopt a structure that paralleled the NFL and the NBA, two of the sporting world's biggest and most successful operations at the time.

Len Coleman, my National League counterpart, and I countered by telling the commissioner that history is one of baseball's greatest assets and that many of its followers would not respond favorably to the change, especially since MLB had recovered from the crippling player strike of 1994 and attendance was reaching record heights.

The commissioner clearly won the argument, and Reinsdorf and several other owners told me later that it was their intent to merge the activities of the leagues while retaining the presidents, in name, as significant staff officers for Selig. The commissioner and his staff were determined to gain control of two highly controversial areas, scheduling and umpires, which remain points of significant contention for owners today.

Jerry Reinsdorf chaired the search committee that recommended me as president of the American League in 1994 after a protracted process. We became friends and allies on many important baseball issues. We are even better friends today, having

Chicago White Sox Photo

An American Success Story
Jerry Reinsdorf celebrated championships
with the Chicago Bulls and the Chicago White Sox.

learned the value of patience and hindsight.

He is an American success story, a kid from Brooklyn who went on to be a lawyer, public accountant, real estate developer, and eventually the owner of the Chicago White Sox and the Chicago Bulls. He has seven world championship rings, one from the 2005 White Sox and six from the Bulls and Michael Jordan during the 1990s. No one else has achieved such a feat.

His parents had a profound influence on him, teaching him the value of truth, fairness, hard work, and boundless enthusiasm and ambition. He never felt poor as a child in Brooklyn, only fortunate to have friends who shared many of his beliefs, ambitions, and sometimes youthful insecurities.

Jackie Robinson was an early idol, showing him firsthand the value of racial diversity and harmony. In Robinson, Reinsdorf saw a stunning athlete who played without fear, refusing to bow to racial insensitivity and numerous inhumane insults.

Robinson strengthened young Reinsdorf's resolve to do what was right, and not necessarily easy, regardless of the color of one's skin and chilling threats from an often unruly crowd. The first African American to break the racial barrier in Major League Baseball was bigger than life to the impressionable Reinsdorf, who marveled at his daring, breathtaking physical skills and feel for the game at legendary Ebbets Field.

Reinsdorf later led successful drives in both professional baseball and basketball to increase the number of minority employees at every level. Then and now, minorities had a special friend in Jerry Reinsdorf, one of the more interesting owners.

He has been the chairman of the White Sox and the Bulls for more than 20 years, and he has witnessed enormous change, especially in baseball, where he has seen forty-five changes in club ownership, seven league presidents, and five commissioners.

During a visit to my economics class in professional sports at Princeton University, Reinsdorf told the students that stable leadership had advantaged the Players Association over the years; it had permitted the association to become professional sports' most powerful union, one that "understood the word take" and "failed to acknowledge the word give." He pointed specifically to the lengthy tours of duty for Marvin Miller and Donald Fehr, who made the owners "easy prey" in the past.

Informed sports columnists such as Murray Chass of the New York Times and Bill Madden of the New York Daily News, who have reported on labor negotiations over the years, agree, believing the tenure issue has impacted the direction of baseball in significant ways, but most dramatically in terms of player salaries. It should be noted that baseball management has substituted freely on its team of negotiators in many past agreement discussions, resulting in a somewhat limited corporate memory. That has changed markedly with the addition of Rob Manfred, one of the commissioner's executive vice presidents who talks with the commissioner regularly, sometimes daily. MLB has regained some ground in the last two bargaining agreements.

Reinsdorf is best described as a liberal on social issues and fiscal conservative among the owners. One of his closest allies is David Glass, the owner of the Kansas City Royals and former CEO of Wal-Mart during its years of greatest growth. They have not cast differing votes on major issues at owners meetings.

Reinsdorf does not anticipate a let up in turnover among the ranks of owners. Too many of them do not understand what they have bought into, or so he believes. He does see more corporate ownership on the horizon, with a much sharper eye on the bottom line. He regards the trend as both good and bad, believing the "suits" will force more fiscal accountability but will lessen the time-honored passion for the game. A growing number of owners are uneasy about this assessment and believe it to be a realistic one.

Reinsdorf believes the ideal owner should be an individual who has a sharp pencil and a passionate love for the game, much as a child does. He believes in revenue sharing to enhance competitiveness, but with clearly defined provisions for its use. It was designed to enhance the "on-field quality for fans, not for ill-defined administrative needs." He takes a dim view of the way a few of his fellow owners have used the funds.

The visitor to my class at Princeton University took care to explain how professional sports teams are significantly different from most other businesses. "In what other business are your competitors your partners?" Reinsdorf asked the class. A high percentage of a team's revenues comes from the actual games, meaning from the competition within the two leagues. For example, the clubs share national television, Internet, and licensing revenues.

Jerry Reinsdorf has a clear and often stated goal as the owner of two major sports franchises. He wants to win championships and at least break even financially. He would rather win and break even than finish second and make $20 million.

Realistically, a big league baseball team has to be considered successful if it finishes in the final four and does not lose money. More and more owners subscribe to the Reinsdorf mantra, believing that any meaningful financial upside will come only when a franchise is sold, and that their ownership is a contribution to the general welfare of a community. Unfortunately, Major League Baseball remains the only reasonably priced professional sport for families.

Chris Young, a student of mine at Princeton and now a pitching star with the San Diego Padres, was struck by the candor of

Reinsdorf and admitted to me that owning an MLB club would be a real challenge and a high-risk business. Chris has an interest in the business of baseball when his playing days are over, seeing it as challenging and an unforgiving high wire act.

An admitted life-long baseball fan, Jerry could not let the rare opportunity pass when the White Sox were put up for sale in February 1981. He formed a syndicate of investors and paid Bill Veeck $19 million for the team on the South Side of Chicago. He does not believe that owning a baseball team is among the better business ventures, although he has "about broken even" with the White Sox.

Revenues of Major League Baseball have grown dramatically in the past 15 to 20 years, but so have the operating expenses and especially the player salaries. Annual revenues for America's pastime will exceed $5.5 billion in 2008. Reinsdorf expends nearly $100 million a year for players, while the 2007 champion Boston Red Sox had a $140 million payroll and the eastern rival New York Yankees spent more than $200 million. The figures are truly stunning for MLB, but so are the figures for the NFL and the NBA.

New owners usually seek out Reinsdorf for an unvarnished discussion of the past and future economic course of the game, leaving no stones unturned during the question and answer segment. They find him unusually candid, extremely well informed, and concerned for the future of the sport that means so much to him and his family. He can be painfully direct, but never personal. A majority of the owners, past and present, regard Jerry as a mentor and friend, as "one of the old guys who knows his stuff."

His influence is pervasive and one needs to understand that he has been an active member of the powerful Executive Council of MLB for two decades. No major policy is recommended to the owners without a thorough vetting by the Executive Council.

Commissioner Selig presides over the council and has a record of being in sync with the members on most compelling issues like the introduction of the wild card, interleague play, increasing balance among teams with economic reforms, and the construction and preservation of fan-friendly ballparks.

Reinsdorf has been an aggressive and highly influential member of the Ownership Committee for years, helping to determine who owns and who sells baseball franchises. Some critics believe he has too much influence on the game and on the commissioner. Some reporters see Reinsdorf and Selig as being joined at the hip, but this is not so. They often disagree, but in private, and they will continue to offer a united front in public. They are friends.

Reinsdorf's fingerprints can be seen on many matters of substance that have been brought before the Board of Directors of the Player Relations Committee. Some players and union members are suspicious of Reinsdorf and his motives, and have been for years. One such critic has been Gene Orza, the number two person at the Players Association and a worthy adversary. Reinsdorf enjoys taking his turn in suggesting labor policy and strategy.

One of his lasting contributions as an owner can be seen through his tireless work as co-chair of the Equal Opportunity Committee, where he has forced open the doors of opportunity for many deserving minorities and women. He led the way for the purchase of millions of dollars in goods and services from minority- and women-owned businesses, and the White Sox always rank among baseball's leaders in the Diverse Business Partners Program.

Without exception, the Northwestern law school graduate and board trustee always credits others for high profile successes in baseball and basketball. He is uncomfortable in the spotlight, but he was especially proud in 2005 when his world champion

White Sox had a Hispanic manager (Ozzie Guillen) and an African American general manager (Ken Williams). His message was unmistakable: Diversity can be a winner on and off the field.

During his long and storied career, Reinsdorf, who calls himself "the luckiest Jew alive," has built two new sports facilities in Chicago—Comiskey Park in 1991, now U.S. Cellular Field, and the United Center in 1994. The new facilities for baseball and basketball are sources of great pride in the state of Illinois.

"Jerry Reinsdorf is one of our most involved and generous citizens," Hall of Fame running back Gale Sayers of the Chicago Bears said. Reinsdorf has given millions of dollars to causes in the Windy City, including city parks, Special Olympics, inner city Little League, and an innovative reading program for public school students. He has played a leadership role in developing the west side area surrounding the United Center and he has introduced countless kids to the joy of participating in sports.

Like most owners of sports enterprises, Jerry has had his share of second-guessers over the years. Some in the press, and more than a few basketball fans, believe he prematurely broke up the championship Bulls, sending the likes of Jordan, Scotty Pippen, and Dennis Rodman elsewhere, while other titles were within their grasp for Chicago. Reinsdorf has disputed the contention for years. Others believed that he did not give proper respect to Bill Veeck, an ever popular figure in Chicago, after the sale of the White Sox. Some among the White Sox following resented his threat to move the team to Florida unless a new Comiskey was built, and a few have never forgiven him for the firing of manager Tony LaRussa, who went on to experience great success with the Athletics and the Cardinals. LaRussa is, by the way, one of Reinsdorf's closest friends.

Owning an entry in the NBA can be far different than

baseball, and it can be quite profitable. In 1985, Reinsdorf bought the Chicago Bulls, then a troubled franchise, and the club has turned a meaningful profit for most of the years since. Reinsdorf was convinced at the time he purchased the Bulls that, with an adopted cap on player salaries in the NBA (something that MLB has not been able to do) and some operational changes, the club could be profitable. His ownership of the Bulls experienced an extraordinary run of success with Michael Jordan and friends.

To fully understand Reinsdorf, a shrewd businessman, you must know that he was born in Brooklyn in 1936. He regarded Brooklyn as the fourth largest city in the United States at the time, not as a part of New York City. He lived and thrived in a place with true diversity—different races, religions, national origins, and political parties. His parents taught him to adapt to most settings.

During Reinsdorf's formative years, baseball was the only real national sport. Neither the NBA nor the NFL had really taken nationwide wings until well after the arrival of Jackie Robinson in 1947. Reinsdorf lived and died with the Dodgers. His parents taught him that discrimination for any reason was wrong and in no one's best interest. He told the students at Princeton that he saw at an early age that all groups had good people and "their share of jerks."

It was Reinsdorf's diverse background that prompted Commissioner Selig and me to ask him to lead baseball's crusade to increase the number of minority employees at every level of the game, both on and off the field of play. It would not be easy. He led the drive with conviction throughout the 1990s, and his efforts resulted in new awareness and tangible hiring progress. Reinsdorf freely criticized those owners who failed to measure up on the minority front. He was never satisfied, insisting that fines be levied on clubs not meeting agreed-upon hiring objectives. He lost friends in the process.

With the force of the commissioner's office, Reinsdorf also pressed the clubs to seek out women and minority-owned businesses, emphasizing that Major League Baseball wanted them to compete for purchases of goods and services. Initially women and minority businesses were skeptical, but the early results were encouraging, with the clubs getting a larger pool of supplies and better quality goods and services at lower prices.

The game was making new and needed friends among the female and minority ranks, and more and more people of color started to attend baseball games during this period of new-found receptivity and trust. Women have always attended MLB games in large numbers. According to Reinsdorf, both minorities and non-minorities are likely to buy your product if they see you as an equal opportunity company and a contributor to the community.

Among his basic rules for success during nearly three decades of ownership: Hire good people, permit them to grow, treat them right, and have the courage to back them during difficult times. The formula works for Jerry.

Jerry Reinsdorf and his wife, Martyl, have four children and seven grandchildren, all of whom enjoy baseball and basketball games. They see the images of sport much like a wide-eyed kid from Brooklyn did generations ago.

an Uncommon
Man

Over the years Bob Kerrey and I have talked about many things
— our native state of Nebraska and the stoic nature of its people,
what has happened to a once-proud Husker football tradition, the
natural beauty of the Sandhills in the fall, the aging process and
how it is affecting us, our many mutual friends, the plight of the
handicapped in modern society, higher education trends and stan-
dards, changing student values, the importance of good writing,
the shifting globalization of the economy, the Beatles, politics, the
war on terror, Iraq, and on and on. Some of our most enjoyable
conversations have taken place at Yankee Stadium over a hot dog
and cold beer.

No one truly knows Kerrey and can claim to be his best friend.
Just when you think you have solved the mystery of Senator Kerrey
he moves on, often in a totally different direction. He can be mys-
terious, but I believe I understand what drives him, if not always
the direction. His unpredictability is part of the puzzle.

Kerrey vividly remembers visiting the White House and receiving the Congressional Medal of Honor. He certainly did not feel
like a hero at the time; he was, in fact, undecided and uneasy
about accepting the decoration, reasoning that so many others
were more deserving and most of them got little recognition, if
any, for their bravery.

He went to Washington, his first trip there, because the Medal
of Honor was important to his parents and family. Members of his

New School University Photo

Medal of Honor Winner
Bob Kerrey, soldier, politician, and university president.

Navy Seal team asked him to accept the recognition, believing it brought honor to many gallant and fallen men and women who served in Vietnam. They had recommended him for the Silver Star and it had been upgraded. He was embarrassed.

Kerrey had turned against the war and most politicians while he was a patient in the Naval Hospital in Philadelphia; he had lost part of a leg. After much study and thought, he saw little justification for continuance of the war. He concluded the only honorable thing to do was end the war, and he believed Richard Nixon was elected in 1968 because he claimed to have a plan to end the conflict with "peace and honor."

While at the White House, Kerrey wished that he could share some of the apparent pride that his parents felt. He was envious, for they had lived in a generation of clarity, a time when they fought a justifiable fight in World War II.

Kerrey recalls wearing an ill-fitting tan navy uniform that accentuated his slight frame. Only the day was bright for the young Seal whose seriously injured leg was throbbing throughout the brief ceremony. The aspirin he took did little to relieve the discomfort of the injury.

President Nixon said little that day other than that the 12 honorees were heroes, part of a heroic cause. Nixon appeared wooden and ashen to Kerrey. Despite reservations, the young man from Nebraska was impressed by the ceremony and the bravery of the other men who were cited that day in May.

A reception for the Medal of Honor awardees and their families followed the ceremony. The president and his daughter, Julie Nixon Eisenhower, were there to shake hands, and neither was especially warm, he thought. Kerrey was ready to go back to Lincoln and a life of anonymity.

There was no one to greet him and offer congratulations for his high military honor when he and his family returned to Lincoln. Only one politician, J. James Exon, even wrote to thank him for his service. At the time, Exon was a Democratic candidate for governor, and he and Kerrey later would bond and become close friends and colleagues in the U. S. Senate.

When he returned to work in the pharmacy at Bryan Memorial Hospital, he and his supervisor and friend, Dr. Oliver Waite, spoke briefly about the White House ceremony. Kerrey once again insisted that others were far more deserving of the honor. War was a topic that made Kerrey uncomfortable when he went back to college, enrolling in accounting and political science courses at the University of Nebraska in Lincoln. Before enlisting in the Navy, he had completed a degree in pharmacy and found comfort in thoughts about a good job and a life free from complications in the Midwest. He loved the openness of the state of Nebraska.

Kerrey joined the Navy in October 1966, convinced of the right of the United States and the value of patriotism. He thought it was an honor to serve one's country, and he believed in the integrity of those vested with elective office. He was intrigued with the thought of being a Navy Seal, one of America's elite forces. Instead of accepting an assignment to the fleet as a junior officer, he was drawn to the challenges of underwater demolition. Kerrey never took the easy road. In many ways, he was a typical young man who romanticized risk and victory.

He was introduced to the brutality of war shortly after his arrival in Vietnam. In his very first firefight, women and children perished, and he had recurring nightmares about the tragic incident. He still does. His second encounter cost him part of his leg and began the erosion of certainty in his long-held beliefs on war and the political process.

Kerrey spent a year in the hospital and experienced unimaginable pain. He drew needed strength from his fellow patients, many of whom were more disabled than he. As he learned to walk again, he realized that pain would be a lifetime companion. He rarely complained during his hospital stay or later in life, and he attributed much of his toughness to his rigorous training as a Navy Seal.

He was released and discharged in December 1969, weighing little more than 140 pounds. He felt ghostlike. He was emotional when he said farewell to his friends and nurses at the hospital, and many of them remain his close friends today. Bob Kerrey had changed, leaving behind some of his lifetime beliefs and values; he felt sobered and betrayed.

He returned home on a military flight to Offutt Air Force Base south of Omaha, refusing an offer to be flown home on a commercial airplane and escorted by his father. He wanted more time to think, to heal, and to adapt. He hitchhiked the last 50 miles to Lincoln in icy weather.

His new wooden leg was painful in the cold and he bled as he walked along the highway. Four college students from Lincoln picked him up and drove him to his home. The driver assured the passenger in the wrinkled uniform that they were in no way against American soldiers, but rather against the conduct of the war. Kerrey remembers returning filled with anger and resentment, and in a quandary about what the right path out of Vietnam might be.

In the years that followed, he was successful in business, operating a chain of restaurants and fitness centers in Lincoln and Omaha from 1972 to 1982. He wanted to do more, and he felt an obligation to make a difference as a public person. He was committed to the handicapped and to economically disadvantaged children.

In 1982 he was elected governor as an unknown Democrat, and upon taking office he inherited a budget deficit and was faced with severe federal cutbacks during a time of national economic hardship. There was little time to dream and be creative. He had to face fiscal reality and bring the deficit under control by chopping the budget. He balanced the state budget in each of his four years as governor and turned the deficit into a comfortable budget surplus.

Young Kerrey gained national attention as a governor who introduced innovative programs in welfare reform, elementary and secondary education, job training, and the environment. Many of his programmatic efforts became national models for innovation and creativity. His logic and rhetoric were compelling to an attentive citizenry. Administrators from the University of Nebraska liked him, but thought he was stingy during his term in office and slowed needed research activity.

As governor, he continually amazed farmers and ranchers with the depth of his knowledge about corn, wheat, milo, milk, hogs, cattle, and poultry. He knew agriculture. He intrigued voters when he dated actress Debra Winger while she was filming Terms of Endearment in Lincoln, a movie that won the 1983 Oscar for Best Motion Picture. The attractive pair caught the national spotlight.

The governor was regarded by most members of the press as a liberal on social issues and a conservative on fiscal matters. Whatever he did seemed to work in the eyes of the electorate.

Kerrey was easily elected to the U. S. Senate in 1988, establishing a liberal voting record on social issues despite the fact that Nebraska was, and remains, one of the most conservative states in the nation. He was tight-fisted with federal tax dollars. The voters from his native state found him different and engaging, unpredictable and refreshing.

Colleagues in the Senate were often frustrated by his unwillingness to commit to votes on critical issues until the last minute. He was fiercely independent and carefully weighed each major piece of legislation. His legislative interests were wide ranging and his approval ratings soared at home. He was a political enigma to many in the national media, a liberal who, for example, voted against abolishing farm subsidies.

As the only member of the Congress to have received the Medal of Honor, America's highest military honor, he was looked to for guidance on intelligence, defense, and military matters. His Senate peers liked and respected him on these and other matters of national concern. He was a celebrity player in Washington.

Many in the national democratic party thought he had presidential appeal, and he believed a race for president would permit him a rare opportunity to force discussion on matters of vital national importance. There was considerable interest in him and his maverick ways, and the national press could not get enough of him as he announced his candidacy in September 1991. He made health care for all one of his first and principal themes. Long lines of energetic young volunteers appeared overnight, reminding many observers of the days of Gene McCarthy and Bobby Kennedy. But the Kerrey campaign was doomed early because of inadequate finances and little professional organization. Bill Clinton was eventually nominated and elected president in 1992.

Bob Kerrey was reelected to the Senate in 1994 and served as chair of the powerful Democratic Senatorial Campaign Committee for the 104th Congress before retiring in 2001. He became recognized as a highly successful fundraiser and a leader to be reckoned with among democratic senators. He was a strong supporter of free trade and limiting the size of the federal budget, and he advocated active diplomacy, foreign aid, and heightened intelligence.

Close personal friends noticed that he was losing enthusiasm for the cumbersome legislative process and was casting an eye for something new, different, and more rewarding.

That quest led him to New York City in 2001 for the presidency of the New School University, an institution known for its liberal history and progressive values. He has initiated an ambitious fund-raising program that is increasing professorships, student scholarships, and needed physical facilities. He continues to do what he believes is right and proper, sometimes riling activist faculty and students. For example, President Kerrey invited former Senate colleagues and close friends John McCain and Joe Lieberman, political moderates, to address high-profile campus events, prompting heated criticism from certain campus groups. The defense of his selections drew editorial support from the major New York newspapers, much to the dismay of angry faculty and students. Kerrey continues to be invigorated by controversy and debate on substantive issues.

He has been asked by several high profile state universities to consider their presidencies, but the answer has been a polite but unequivocal no. He likes where he is. He is married to Sarah Paley and they have a son, Henry. He has children from a previous marriage, Ben and Lindsey.

One must return to Bob Kerrey's youth at Lincoln Northeast High School to begin to understand him. He was an undersized member of the football team and earned the starting position as center in his senior year while weighing only 155 pounds. He believed that "size of the heart matters in things of importance," on and off of the playing field. He thrived on being an underdog in high school football as he did in gaining election as a governor and a member of the U.S. Senate. His nose, permanently scarred by the charges of opposing linemen, constantly reminded him of the importance of courage and perseverance.

"No sacrifice is too great for one's country and one's beliefs," he told me at the New School. "America remains an international beacon for millions of men and women, and we must be deserving of that trust in the years ahead." He lost part of a leg in Vietnam, but not his combative spirit. He believes the average person is capable of extraordinary things if properly motivated and directed.

As a member of the National Commission on Terrorist Attacks upon the United States (popularly known as the "9/11 Commission"), he was highly critical of republicans and democrats, and he has questioned the actions of President George W. Bush and former New York mayor Rudy Giuliani. His work on the Commission won praise from many in the press.

In 2001, the New York Times Magazine and 60 Minutes carried reports on an incident that occurred during Kerrey's service. On February 25, 1969, he led a raid on an isolated village where a Viet Cong leader was supposed to be present. The village was considered part of a free-fire zone by the U.S. military.

Kerrey's Seal team encountered a peasant house, or hooch, and killed the people inside. Although Kerrey said he did not go inside the hooch and participate in the killings, another member of the team said he had. The people killed were an elderly man and woman and three children.

Despite differing recollections, Kerrey accepts responsibility for the tragedy as the team leader. There was a brief public outcry for an investigation, but Vietnam War heroes democrat John Kerry and republican John McCain dismissed the call and supported their former colleague in the Senate. Kerrey has expressed anguish and regret over the event on numerous occasions.

After the burst of media attention, Kerrey and the six men he led that night met and compared individual memories. There were some inconsistencies, but they were in agreement over the most important details. War is often imprecise and always torturous, as most veterans know.

Despite years of high-profile success, Bob Kerrey, my valued friend, remains haunted by the memories of war, memories that never seem to quite escape him. Vietnam cost him his innocence, a loss of solace in his religion, and his basic health. Like so many others, he suffered years of disillusionment.

More than ever, the former senator from the Midlands is committed to an America free from war and resulting death. He regards the prosecution of the war in Iraq as mismanaged, believing it to be, in large measure, the result of a reckless foreign policy concocted by a circle of people without vision who controlled the White House. He sees war as the ultimate failure, and he intends to continue to speak out on the issues of the day when he feels that it is warranted. He does believe in the importance of enhanced diplomacy and a strong national defense. I believe the country is better because of his often-seen independence of thought and action.

The Big
Score

Al Neuharth always loved baseball, believing that he had the managerial skills to make it to "The Bigs," whether in sports or somewhere else. He never doubted himself. Rather, he thrived on challenge. To really understand him you have to turn the clock back.

At the age of 19, the self-described poor kid from "the wrong side of the tracks" was a member of the U.S. 86th Infantry Division serving in World War II. The Army deployed him to both Europe and the Pacific, where he learned the importance of discipline, courage, and trust.

Neuharth vividly remembers meeting General George S. Patton, Jr., near Heidelberg, Germany, as the war was winding down. It impacted the way he viewed many things. Then a staff sergeant assigned to an intelligence and reconnaissance platoon, he was marching two dozen captured German soldiers to a prison camp for interrogation. He and the captives had stopped for a brief rest when Patton spotted them.

According to Neuharth, the general jumped from his Jeep and shouted to him to get on his feet or "you will be behind the same barbed wire as the prisoners." The startled soldier from South Dakota snapped to attention, saluted, and moved on with dispatch. He respected Patton, seeing him as a real life hero, one who always won by never resting or underestimating the enemy.

After Victory in Europe Day (VE Day), the 86th Division

returned to the states and was hailed in a parade down Fifth
Avenue in New York City. Neuharth saw first-hand how winning
brought inner satisfaction and widespread recognition. He real-

A Journalistic Giant

Allen H. Neuharth, founder of USA TODAY,
America's most widely read newspaper.

ized that nothing of real value comes easy and there is no substitute for victory.

He returned to his native state of South Dakota after the war and enrolled in college, deciding to pursue a degree in journalism at the University of South Dakota. He enjoyed campus politics and work on the student newspaper more than his studies. Even at a young age he delighted in tweaking the establishment, discovering the power of the press in all segments of campus life.

He registered his first big failure at age 29 when he launched a weekly statewide sports tabloid for all of South Dakota. The contents of the publication were good, but the business plan was not. He learned much and recommitted himself to further runs at success. He never indulged in self pity. Thirty years later he would introduce USA TODAY.

Little league failures would lead to big league successes, Neuharth reasoned. He proved that he could sprint with the best of them in the cut-throat business of big-time journalism, with highly successful managerial stops at the Miami Herald and the Detroit Free Press.

These were dream jobs for the ambitious young man from Alpena, South Dakota. He was given increasing responsibility, high visibility, and the opportunity to learn about the business without losing regular contact with the newsroom. It was at these stops that he honed the competitive skills he would need to climb the often unforgiving corporate ladder.

Neuharth admittedly had more fun in Miami, but he learned how to play hardball in Detroit, clashing with people like Jimmy Hoffa and the Teamsters. He always took time to have fun, considering a good joke essential to his well being.

Neuharth caught the attention of the Gannett Company, then a relatively small but profitable organization operating out of

Rochester, New York, with 16 newspapers averaging 50,000 in circulation. He was growing bored in Detroit and needed to reinvent himself with something new and different. He believed Gannett was ripe for growth outside of the Northeast, and he saw himself as the person who could pull it off, as the person who could manage the newspaper chain from the minors to the big leagues. His instincts were correct.

He began as operating head of the Rochester Times-Union and Democrat and Chronicle, with a combined circulation of 263,665. He was a proactive executive, writing occasional headlines in the newsroom, making random sales calls with advertising staff, and visiting the pressroom late at night to check the quality of printing. Nothing of moment escaped his sharp eye. The results were obvious, circulation went up nicely, and annual earnings increased by more than a third. At age 41, he was a rising star at Gannett and a person to be reckoned with.

He and then Gannett chairman Paul Miller had serious designs on the state of Florida, hoping to launch a new kind of daily newspaper there, one filled with creative stories, lively writing, and rich color. Miller saw an added advantage of being able to play more golf in the Florida sunshine. Neuharth was encouraged by Gannett's willingness to gamble at a time when many daily newspapers across the country were dying on the vine. The newspaper industry was struggling in the 1950s and 60s. While many were ringing their hands, Neuharth saw only opportunity.

He cast an eye on Florida's Space Coast for the new newspaper, realizing there would be formidable competition from newspapers in Miami, Orlando, Daytona Beach, and Tampa. It would not be easy. He first commissioned newspaper-reader research, which showed Space Coast residents were newcomers who loved new and different ideas—new frontiers, if you will. The research also revealed that the residents were from places other than Florida, and their interests were global. The timing was right.

The new newspaper would be called TODAY, and it had a first year circulation goal of 20,000. It doubled that figure after just 12 months. An investment of less than $10 million would result in a newspaper valued at more than $200 million after 20 years of publication. The challenging venture resulted in one of the finest newspapers of its size in the United States.

Al Neuharth rose from a reporter to a corporate president in 16 years, but he had only started. Other major newspapers were intrigued with Neuharth and his way of doing business. The New York Daily News, then the largest daily newspaper in the country, with a circulation of 2.1 million, was actively interested in having him run their publication. He won points with Gannett by staying, preferring to battle for the CEO position that he eventually got.

Neuharth was driven to create USA TODAY, a publication that would give him and Gannett a deserved national voice of influence. He thought too many major newspapers were controlled by heirs, not self-made doers. He felt that Gannett was treated by newspaper elitists as "a country bumpkin" even though it was the biggest newspaper company in America in 1980. He was especially spurred on by the owners and attitudes of editors at the New York Times and the Washington Post. Neuharth believed, as never before, that "fortune favors the bold."

During his years as CEO, the Gannett Company acquired 69 daily newspapers, 16 television stations, 29 radio stations, and North America's largest outdoor sign business. He made mistakes, some of them big ones. His finest hour came on September 15, 1982, when Gannett introduced USA TODAY, the first national, general-interest daily newspaper.

It was truly his newspaper and a crowning achievement, most

agreed. Celebrating the launch with Al Neuharth in Washington, DC, was the president of the United States, the Speaker of the House, and the Senate majority leader. Senators and representatives, cabinet members, and local and state officials were everywhere, mingling with some 800 guests.

Ronald Reagan, Thomas "Tip" O'Neill, and Howard Baker were there to offer praise, while many in the profession hoped to see the new publication fail. The founder of USA TODAY had his detractors, and there were more than a few.

The average reader liked what he saw in the new publication— a newspaper with short, well-written news and feature stories, and a lot of color. There were four sections—national and international news, money, sports, and life. A popular feature was the large color weather map of the United States. USA TODAY was a high-tech, satellite delivered newspaper, even though Neuharth claimed to know little about such technological advancements.

Staid media types called the newspaper "McPaper," implying that it was mere junk-food journalism. Readers, however, liked USA TODAY, and the members of the Board of Directors at Gannett saw enormous potential. USA TODAY, with a circulation of nearly 2.3 million daily, was started in 1982 and became profitable in just five years. It was suddenly America's most widely read newspaper.

Dolph Simons, Jr., publisher of the Lawrence, Kansas, Journal-World, introduced me to Al Neuharth when I was chancellor of the University of Kansas in the early 1980s. Neuharth was in Lawrence, Kansas, to announce that the Journal-World would be printing USA TODAY for much of the Midwest. That agreement is still in force today.

What I remember about Neuharth was his fashionably late entrance, complete with an impressive entourage of professionals from USA TODAY. The troop had a rock star presence that I found a little over the top for a sleepy university town. But it was great fun.

Neuharth proved to be insightful, clever, and a bit of a showman. He mixed with ease, responding to any and all questions from those in attendance. He took time to talk with me about the storied history of journalism education at the University of Kansas and the long-standing success of Jayhawk men's basketball. Neuharth was a bit shorter than I thought he would be; he was my height, five foot, eight inches. People small in stature are often driven to overcompensate, or so I have found. They often have something to prove.

He seemed ego driven, but in a nonintrusive way. He was the picture of competitiveness, welcoming the opportunity to battle with the country's biggest and best newspapers. He smiled when asked about the possible outcome. He dressed expensively, like a media mogul should.

It was apparent that Neuharth wanted to be recognized for his many achievements at Gannett. Years later, at a World Series game in Cleveland, we talked about the leaders of the media world who were in place because of birth. He liked to talk about what he had to do to reach the pinnacle of success, never showing a trace of rancor, but merely citing the importance of imagination, vision, salesmanship, and hard work.

Neuharth and I have become good friends over the past 25 years. We have attended quite a few Major League Baseball games together, talked newspaper trends on numerous occasions, and shared a friendship with George Steinbrenner, the sometimes unpredictable owner of the New York Yankees. Al writes at least once a year that Steinbrenner is baseball's best owner because he is committed to providing New York with winning baseball regardless of the cost to him. As chairman of the board of The News-

Gazette newspaper at Champaign, Illinois, I especially enjoy talking with Neuharth about media ethics and responsibilities.

It should be pointed out that Neuharth has thoroughly enjoyed competing with the biggest names in publishing—names like Sulzberger, Chandler, Cowles, and Graham. He believes his winning percentage would keep him on any major league team, and he always played the game his way.

USA TODAY has triggered many changes in the newspaper business. Most profitable papers now use many of the ideas introduced by the Gannett flagship publication, such as shorter and crisper news stories, more color, many more pictures, increased sports coverage, clever headlines, quality newsprint, and attention-grabbing vending boxes.

"Al used new technology to produce a better newspaper and new satellite technology to distribute constantly updated news to print sites around the country," Dolph Simons said. "USA TODAY readers get the latest and that is critical in an area like sports where games are often finished late at night."

Neuharth also knew which sections of the country would be most receptive to the new newspaper. He carefully picked his fights and usually won. Many of his early critics now believe he created something very special and lifted the bar of expectations for daily newspapers. They often compare him with Ted Turner and his creative ventures into cable news. No two people, I contend, have made a greater impact on the delivery of news in the past six decades than Neuharth and Turner.

Perhaps his greatest contribution to the newspaper industry receives little attention. It was the flamboyant journalist from the hills of South Dakota who bought needed time for America's newspapers to become both relevant and attractive, to become truly competitive with cable, television, and the Internet. He made the printed word attractive to millions of readers, even to the young. He proved that his old manual Royal typewriter and keen business mind were capable of extraordinary heights.

Interestingly, the two innovators—Neuharth and Turner—are not close friends, but each respects the other and what each has achieved against heavy odds. In so many ways, they were alike. Neuharth once told a class of mine at Princeton University that "creative risk takers are the ones who fill the pages of history." He cited the creativity of Ted Turner. He told the students at the Ivy League school that the central components of the Gannett Company experiment with a national newspaper were colorful and tightly edited sections dealing with national news, editorial views, business, entertainment, and sports.

He said virtually every daily newspaper of size has followed, some reluctantly, his format for success; he believed that "no newspaper could survive long without an informative and attractive sports section." Time has proven Neuharth correct on most counts, and he was named the most influential person in print media for the 1990s by the Washington Journalism Review (now the American Journalism Review).

He retired from Gannett in 1989 at age 65, despite protests from his board of directors. During his lengthy tenure with the company, annual revenues increased from $200 million to $3.1 billion. The company had 21 years of uninterrupted earnings gains. He left on top, unlike many professional baseball players. Gannett had become the biggest newspaper company in the United States, USA TODAY had become the country's most read newspaper, and the next generation of leadership was in place.

In 1991 Neuharth founded one of the nation's largest private charitable foundations, the Freedom Forum, which was the successor to the Gannett Foundation, established in 1935 by Frank E.

Gannet. Neuharth used his new pulpit to challenge newspapers everywhere to be worthy of public trust, to remember the common good of society. He resented passive journalism in any form and liked to zero in on the ethics of the profession.

He retired for a second time on June 1, 1997, only to continue to stir the waters of controversy as a frequent guest on national talk shows, including those hosted by Oprah Winfrey, Larry King, David Letterman, and Bob Costas.

He continues to rile audiences from across the country and abroad with lectures on business, government, media, and academia. His weekly column in USA TODAY and other Gannett newspapers reaches some 22 million readers, and it can be both folksy and biting. He freely offers space for one sentence rebuttals and defenses from friends and foes alike. He has frequently criticized President George W. Bush for his foray into Iraq, calling as early as December of 2004 for American troops to be brought home.

Neuharth is married to Dr. Rachel Fornes, a chiropractor in Cocoa Beach, Florida. She is his third wife and they have six adopted children.

There is much to admire about Allen H. Neuharth, but even he has described himself in the past as an S.O.B. He can be abrasive and charming, complex and direct, tightfisted and generous. He can be self-absorbed and yet sympathetic to the needs of the less fortunate. He often defies labels, which frustrates many of his critics in the media world. I simply accept him for what he is, a good friend with many admirable traits, ones that more of us should try to emulate.

Country
Comes First

Most people know Bob Dole as an American statesman, as one whose influence was felt on virtually every major decision made in the U. S. Congress for three decades. He was the longtime senator from Kansas, the 15th Senate majority leader, republican vice presidential candidate in 1976, and presidential nominee of the republicans in 1996. He made things happen in Washington and elsewhere.

Historians will remember his unique effectiveness as a consensus-builder and, unlike a growing number of today's legislators, he understood the fundamental and essential role of reasoned compromise on the difficult issues. He always did his homework and was known for his patience with, and respect for, colleagues from both sides of the aisle. Some observers have likened Dole to Lyndon B. Johnson when he served as majority leader of the Senate. It is a fair comparison. Both senators had deep rural roots, got big things done for the country, and did so with civility.

Senator Dole's associates and friends came from both political parties, individuals such as republicans Howard Baker of Tennessee and John Warner of Virginia and democrats like John Glenn of Ohio and Edward Kennedy of Massachusetts. They fiercely argued the challenges of the time, but always concluded with a handshake and personal feelings in tact. They were leaders in the best sense of the word, leaders who knew when it was time to come together and act in the best interests of the nation.

Lawrence Journal-World Photo

American Statesman
Bob Dole, World War II hero
and champion for the disabled in America.

As a youngster in Russell, Kansas, Bob dreamed of becoming a medical doctor and serving the health needs of the community in which he was raised. His parents were good citizens, working long and hard hours to support their family, and they freely encouraged young Bob to pursue his dream at the University of Kansas. His mother told him not to worry about the money; it would be found when necessary.

With a summer of savings and a loan from the local banker, Bob was off to Lawrence to pursue his goals. He immediately liked the students and the spacious green lawns on campus. He quickly landed a job as a waiter to lessen the burden at home. He once admitted to me that he was "more than a little intimidated" by the size of the university.

He made the freshman football team and still remembers how "tough those varsity guys were." He also made the basketball and track teams at KU. The senator reminded me more than once during my tenure as chancellor of the University of Kansas that a "winning tradition in athletics" was of real importance to alumni and friends of the school. He was especially proud when the Jayhawks won the national basketball championship in 1988.

One of his university friends gave him a suit for social occasions, but it never fit right; the pants were "too big in the seat." While at college, Bob wrote home often asking for any and all information about Russell. He could not get enough news about the community and the people there. He treasured the letters from his parents, his brother, and his two sisters, and he read the contents over and over.

His life would soon change forever as he joined an army of young men and women who believed they had a responsibility to fight for their country and what it stood for in World War II. Bob enlisted in 1942, was called up in 1943, and by early 1945 was on duty in the cold and rugged mountains of Italy. He always saw himself as an average guy, like the other soldiers around him. He wanted to be liked and respected, and he was.

As a second lieutenant he led dangerous patrols at night, watching for German snipers and possible enemy movements that might threaten American troops. Young Dole and his men drew strength from Franklin D. Roosevelt, who was a courageous leader despite being crippled by polio. Dole remembers April 12, 1945, when the president died. Many soldiers in the foxholes openly wept with the announcement and thoughts of life without FDR were troubling to many.

The Americans launched a massive assault on well-fortified German positions a few days later (April 14) and casualties were heavy. Lieutenant Dole and his troops were ordered to take what their map simply called Hill 913, a steep mound of earth. It would prove to be a bloody undertaking. "Stuff was coming at us from every direction," he recalled.

The 21-year-old soldier from Russell was hit by enemy fire in his shoulder and back while attempting to pull his radio man to safety. His injuries were life threatening. He would lose a kidney and the use of his right arm, and most of the feeling and strength in his left arm. He also suffered a severe spinal injury that left him paralyzed for many months.

He immediately realized that he would not be going home anytime soon, that his days as a student athlete at the University of Kansas were probably over, and that his dreams of being the town physician were not to be. He did take comfort in knowing that he had formed a lifetime bond with his men and that would help him through the painful days ahead.

Significantly, Russell was to become even more important to the injured Bob Dole. I remember hearing him talk about the beauty of the "blue skies over town in the spring and in the fall." He especially liked the limestone homes and buildings, the changing of the seasons, the cleanliness of his home, the clothes his mother made for his sisters, and how everybody called each other by a first name. He saw his mother as a saint. Hearing the senator reminisce reminded me of my own home town in southwest Nebraska. Russell and McCook were about the same size and were made up of loving families with high values and a deep faith in the Lord.

The senator spent 39 months in military hospitals, places where he had countless hours to think about what might have been. He was, at times, dispirited by his inability to do much of anything, and sometimes he felt trapped by a keen and pervasive sense of helplessness. But his spirits were lifted when he was transferred to Percy Jones Army Hospital in Battle Creek, Michigan, a place where seriously injured soldiers thought miracles could happen. Bob certainly wanted to believe that. PJAH was nationally known for its sensitive care for patients and its rehabilitative work with disabled military people who were trying to reclaim their lives. The staff of doctors and nurses was among the best to be found anywhere.

During his time in Michigan there were numerous emotional and physical highs and lows. Once Dole neared death, but his determination to live prevailed. It was here that he met Phyllis Holden, a young graduate from the University of New Hampshire, who would help change the course of his life. She taught new rehabilitative skills at PJAH with knowledge and zeal, and she would become Mrs. Bob Dole.

Dole grew to enjoy trading stories with his fellow patients as he progressed. He liked to laugh. He especially enjoyed the parade of Hollywood stars that came to the hospital to entertain and lift spirits, figures like Gene Autry, Jack Benny, and Bob Hope. He kept in touch with some of them in later years.

Importantly, the wards at Percy Jones gave the Kansan noticeably improved health and exceptional friends, like Daniel Inouye of Hawaii and Phil Hart of Michigan who would join Dole one day as influential members of the U. S. Senate. They were forever linked by a bond forged through common suffering and understanding.

Bob Dole had his final physical examination at Percy Jones on May 14, 1948. The man who had earned two Bronze Stars with an oak-leaf cluster and two Purple Hearts was now retired from the U.S. Army with the rank of captain. He was ready to step into a new world, realizing that it would be both daunting and exciting.

Dole returned to his source of lifelong strength, Russell. There the people freely opened their hearts and their pockets to support him in his decision to study law at Washburn Municipal University at Topeka, the state capital. Fortunately, as Dole would point out, successful lawyers depend on their heads, not their hands or arms. It should be noted that at Dawson's Drugstore, where Bob worked in high school, there was a cigar box in which friends from the community contributed dollars to support the injured soldier with medical and law school expenses. Dole would never forget them and their unconditional support.

Bob Dole proved to be an excellent college student, earning an undergraduate degree in history and a graduate degree in law at Washburn. He studied day and night, driven by the joy of learning. Phyllis was an essential ally, accompanying him to classes and taking notes and transcribing his scribbles. Bob often sought out his professors to better understand the substance of their classes, especially in law.

The former Army officer learned something else about himself on the Washburn campus; he realized that he now had an inner strength to meet any and all difficult challenges. While in law school, a friend from Russell who was county attorney urged Dole to run for the state legislature. He eventually ran and won as a republican, and not because of partisan motives. Few democrats won elections in those days in western Kansas and that was reason enough for the aspiring and pragmatic young man to register as a republican.

In 1952, Dole announced his candidacy for Russell county attorney and was elected to four terms, serving until 1960. His record was exceptional as county attorney; he went on to win a close election to the House of Representatives from the sprawling Sixth District and he would be reelected to the House in 1962, 1964, and 1966.

In 1986, Frank Carlson, the longtime senator from Kansas, decided to step aside and Dole quickly entered the race and won the primary and general elections. He was the junior senator from Kansas in November, 1968, and he was reelected in 1974, 1980, 1988, and 1992.

The soldier turned politician reached the pinnacle of leadership in the party of Abraham Lincoln. Then president Richard Nixon asked him to use his considerable skills as chairman of the Republican National Committee in 1972. He remained stoic during the early days of the Watergate crisis. Impressed with his cool under fire, Gerald Ford asked Dole to join him on the national republican presidential ticket in 1976. They lost to Jimmy Carter and Walter Mondale. Only 11,000 votes in the states of Hawaii and Ohio would have changed the outcome.

Another major opportunity came to the senator in 1984 when his friend and colleague, Howard Baker, resigned to join the Reagan White House as chief of staff. Dole was elected to replace him as Senate Majority Leader. His skills as a legislator were widely known and respected on The Hill, and he continued as Senate Minority Leader when the democrats regained control of the Senate four years later.

Billionaire Philip Anschutz of Denver was born in Russell and he regarded Dole as "his role model growing up." He saw the senator as "a Kansan of courage and integrity, a man who dedicated himself to making our world a better place." Wichita business leaders held Bob Dole in the highest regard. "The man went through hell as a soldier and he lived to tell about it. His story is a compelling one," banker Jordan Haines said. Aeronautics executive Russ Meyer agreed, adding, "I've never seen a person with greater skills in bringing people together. He was a remarkable leader who never carried a grudge."

Dole and Phyllis Holden divorced in 1972 and she remarried in 1974. Their daughter, Robin, enjoys a special relationship with her father.

The senator married Elizabeth Hanford Dole in 1975. She has had a remarkable career in public service as a cabinet secretary in the administrations of Ronald Reagan and George H. W. Bush, and as president of the American Red Cross. She was elected to the U.S. Senate from her native state of North Carolina in 2002. Elizabeth and Bob wrote a book together in 1988, *The Doles: Unlimited Partners,* with Richard Norton Smith.

Representatives of the Washington press corps, among the most difficult and jaded anywhere, always enjoyed Bob Dole for his disarming candor and halting wit. They sought him out frequently for formal and off-the-record exchanges. They respected the intellectual strength of the senator from the Plains, mindful of his stature among modern day political figures and his place in American history.

Some historians have been slow, however, to forgive Dole for his harsh words in the heated 1976 presidential election against Jimmy Carter. They, and a number of newspaper pundits who followed the campaign, saw him as mean spirited and vindictive. Some likened him to a hatchet man. He has admitted that he was "over the top" at times, as he and Gerald Ford clearly assumed good and bad cop roles.

To some he was an enigma, but to those who worked with him in the Congress he was one to be counted on. With ease he rose above partisan politics when the issue was central to the nation's well being. He was, by all accounts, an extraordinary legislator, especially on difficult international issues. He shared the values of another prominent Kansan, President Dwight D. Eisenhower. Both were pragmatic centrists.

Ronald Reagan spoke volumes when he said of Bob Dole as Senate Majority Leader, "His title of Leader is not just a job title; it's a description of the man." As one of 18 individuals to serve in the majority leader's role, Dole won widespread praise from both democrats and republicans in the mid-1980s. The Congressional Quarterly observed that the senator "proved a point that badly needed proving at the time: the Senate could be led." In a Wall Street Journal poll, Dole was voted the most effective Senate Majority Leader in the past 25 years.

Like his Midwestern colleague in the Senate, Medal of Honor winner Bob Kerrey, he suffered serious injury while in the defense of his country. Kerrey was a member of the Navy Seals in Vietnam. "Bob Dole knew the face and pain of war," Kerrey, a neighbor from Nebraska, said. "We shared a special and lasting friendship."

As the republican presidential nominee in 1996, Bob Dole was portrayed as an honorable leader, one who had earned his stripes as a powerful senator and effective legislator. His credentials were acknowledged and respected by editorial pages most everywhere.

He eventually lost to democrat Bill Clinton.

It is interesting to point out that Dole became enormously popular with millions of Americans after his defeat. His self-effacing humor was a national hit on late night television. He appeared on the Late Show with David Letterman, Saturday Night Live, the Tonight Show with Jay Leno, Late Night with Conan O'Brien, and the Daily Show with Jon Stewart. He also scored big in national ratings with a series of television commercials. Dole enjoyed sharing his light side.

What is most startling to me is that many observers do not realize the numerous pieces of legislation that Bob Dole shepherded for the disabled in the U. S. Senate. Looking at a long line of wheelchairs at a University of Kansas dedication of a special education building bearing his name, the senator said to me, "All these folks want is to be accepted, to be treated as human beings." His words were underscored by a masked tear or two. Known for his candor, wit, and legislative mastery, Bob Dole should be best remembered for his compassion.

His first speech on the Senate floor was an impassioned plea to improve the lives of the handicapped. He later said, "For too long, disabled people have felt like outcasts. Even well-intentioned family members sometimes do not know what they should do, or not do." It has been more than 60 years since the senator was able to raise his right hand over his head; he knows and feels the pain of the handicapped every day.

Doctoral dissertations and scholarly papers have scrutinized the Dole record in Congress, but, in my judgment, a certain few pieces of legislation need to be cited if one is to really understand Dole's values and ability to work with members of both political persuasions.

He and democrat George McGovern of South Dakota worked

together in the late 1970s and 80s to bring about vital food programs like food stamps, school lunch, school breakfast, and the
WIC (Women, Infants, and Children) Program. WIC assists low
income families in obtaining food needed by infants and young
people. Dole often called McGovern his "partner and friend."

Even today the two former presidential nominees and war veterans are working side by side on a program that would give an
estimated 300 million children worldwide at least one meal a day.
Congress has named the creative initiative the "McGovern-Dole
International School Lunch Program." The United States will ex-
pend between 250 and 300 million dollars a year, believing other
nations will soon follow suit.

The senator from rural America was an active leader in the
passage of farm bills for 35 years, and he was a clear and influential voice on the Senate Agriculture Committee for more than 27
years. He never forgot the farmer and his place in assuring the
nation's well being.

Dole and Senator Patrick Moynihan, a democrat from New
York, brought colleagues together to pass the Social Security
Amendment of 1983 that permitted millions of Americans to re-
ceive their checks on time. He and his Senate colleagues from
both political parties, by working together, saved Social Security.
Dole takes understandable pride when talking about the passage of the Americans with Disabilities Act in 1990, another historic piece of legislation that gained essential bipartisan support.
Senators such as Orrin Hatch of Utah, Tom Harkin of Iowa, and
Ted Kennedy of Massachusetts teamed with Dole in getting the
legislation through, and the sweeping measure gave civil rights
to some 50 million disabled persons, 15 million of those with
severe impairments.

Senators Dole and Kennedy managed the Martin Luther King

Holiday Bill in 1983, and some reporters called them the "political odd couple." In fact, Dole had voted for every civil rights bill starting in 1964.

He joined with another prominent democrat senator and former cabinet member Abraham Ribicoff of Connecticut in 1991, to persuade colleagues to pass the Hospice Care Bill of 1981, a bill that allowed the terminally ill to die with dignity. It was hailed by many in the media as an insightful piece of legislation.

Realizing the importance of creating new jobs and closing major loopholes that unfairly favored big business, Dole played leadership roles in passing the Tax Reform Acts of 1981, 1982, and 1984. He chaired the powerful Senate Finance Committee for several years in the early 1980s.

His imprint can be found on numerous measures of significance impacting foreign and defense policy from 1968 to 1996. He always kept an open mind as he worked with individuals like Joe Lieberman of Connecticut and John McCain of Arizona. Health care was always near the top of his Senate agenda for attention and action.

Several memorable things happened to the senator on January 17, 1997, when he visited at the White House. President Clinton, once a political rival, presented Dole with the Presidential Medal of Freedom, the nation's highest civilian award, permitting him to join former presidents Ronald Reagan, Jimmy Carter, Lyndon B. Johnson, and Gerald Ford in receiving the coveted citation. After the ceremony, Clinton showed Dole a model of the proposed National World War II War Memorial and asked him to chair the memorial campaign.

Not surprisingly, he said yes, reasoning that he could not miss an opportunity to honor the men and women with whom he had served. He immediately remembered the nearly half million

American soldiers who had died and the more than half million who were wounded on the battlefields. It was past time for a grateful nation to express appreciation through a memorial.

It would prove to be a massive undertaking, with patriotic business leaders like Fred Smith, the able CEO of FedEx, giving essential assistance to the senator. Nearly $200 million was eventually raised from more than 600,000 contributors, from corporate executives, average citizens, and families who wanted to honor their loved ones who had served in the war that was to end all wars.

The imposing structure was dedicated on Memorial Day weekend 2004 and Bob Dole was the principal speaker. He sat with 55 Medal of Honor winners, actor Tom Hanks, and broadcaster Tom Brokaw, who did much to make the day possible. The massive crowd on the Washington Mall applauded after the humble man from Russell, Kansas, said, "What we dedicate today is not a memorial to war. Rather it is a tribute to the physical and moral courage that makes heroes out of farm and city boys, and inspires Americans in every generation to lay down their lives for people they will never meet, for ideals that make life itself worth living." Brokaw used the title "The Greatest Generation" to describe those who had served in World War II, and he saw Senator Dole as a deserving representative of that generation. I wholeheartedly agree, and further believe that Bob Dole transcends the generations of Americans with lasting grace and honor.

Perhaps Dole's greatest contribution to those who will follow in the halls of Congress is his time-honored formula for success in government: Be thoroughly prepared, always be respectful of others, be patient, remember consistency often breeds trust, be willing to compromise, always search for reasonable consensus, be willing to share credit with colleagues, and be willing to act even when it is unpopular to do so. What democracies like ours need are men and women capable of creative thought, reasoned answers, and courage to act in face of public criticism. The Dole formula works, but it seems to be used less and less in today's quick-fix political environment, an atmosphere driven too often by opinion polls rather than conviction.

Parting Thoughts

Like few others of their era, these nine strong-willed people understood the value of the ring, and what its acquisition might mean to them and their effectiveness as leaders.

The ring was a powerful objective in their lives, one they hoped would bring lasting, deserved joy and recognition to their families, friends, and communities, one that would bring long-term credibility to them and to their professions. It would, they thought, open doors of opportunity for those men and women who would follow in their professional footsteps. It was the ultimate in their collective eye, the big leagues of life, though they never talked about it in those words.

Their paths to the zenith often appeared insurmountable, brimming with obstacles, challenges, and great personal peril, but they never lost sight of the true objective, the end game.

Without question, this team of nine exceptional players had energized and focused intellect and the tools to persevere and advance in hostile environments. They all resented the term defeat.

They often changed directions, strategies, and game plans, but never lost the will to excel at the highest level. Many over the years criticized them and thought them to be unrealistic dreamers. Some even laughed in a disparaging way at their efforts.

On the way to the circle of victors, all of them experienced painful setbacks. Some were physical, some were personal, and some were financial, but most other people would have found these obstacles to be game-ending or perhaps even terminal.

Despite views to the contrary, these unique individuals were poised and persistent, waiting for the right moment to leave their imprint. Each dared to lead at difficult times while most others were willing to watch and follow.

All of them were influenced by their parents and never forgot their origins. As they have grown older, they often refer to the ways of family and to their roots. They find it reassuring and refreshing to visit their hometowns and old school friends with growing regularity. Without question, they are proud survivors who see the value of what they have achieved.

Of course they all would do some things differently today. They would be better organized, for one, and most said they would have somewhat longer fuses. By their own admission, they were young and impatient.

Each of them wishes that far greater attention would have been given to opening the gates of opportunity for people of color. The slowness on the affirmative action front stunted America's growth and opportunities, they believe. They especially applaud the gains of women in the past two decades.

All are self-proclaimed patriots, believing in the might and potential of the United States of America. They all have imposing records in helping with the advancement of elementary, secondary, and higher education. They are some of the nation's most generous givers.

Professional sports organizations in America have been, for example, among the earliest and strongest supporters of classroom teachers. They favor needed educational change and improvement in the classroom as ways for the young to better compete on the international scene. The same can be said of our chosen teammates from other areas, such as the media, government, and politics.

All believe that the country cannot live in isolation, explaining the determination of professional sports to spread its wings globally. Furthermore, virtually all of the most important pieces of national legislation have an international aspect to them, as they should.

What is certain: Our magical nine, despite noticeable shortcomings, will leave a legacy of huge shoes to fill in the years ahead. The ring is the least we can award them.

Most of them remain contrarians, but in an open and usually positive way. They enjoy mixing it up with bright youngsters, and they want to continue to give to the common good and to their chosen professional fields. Clearly, the competitive spirit they have engendered for generations has made the nation great, and that spirit is very much alive among our young today.

Gene A. Budig

about the Author

A recognized academic leader and writer, Gene A. Budig is the distinguished professor and senior presidential advisor of the College Board in New York City. As the head of three major state universitites, Illinois State University, West Virginia University, and the University of Kansas, he was responsible for the educational programs of 520,000 students. The University of Nebraska graduate served as president of Major League Baseball's American League (1994-2000) and oversaw a period of historic growth in attendance and physical facilities.

READINGS

Babcock, Mike. Heart of a Husker, Tom Osborne's Nebraska Legacy. Champaign, IL: Sports Publishing L.L.C., 2006.

Budig, Gene A. A Game of Uncommon Skill. Westport, CT: Oryx Press, 2002.

Budig, Gene A. The Inside Pitch ... And More. Morgantown, WV: West Virginia University Press, 2004.

Costas, Bob. Fair Ball, A Fan's Case for Baseball. New York: Broadway Books, 2000.

Dole, Bob. One Soldier's Story. New York: HarperCollins, 2005.

Kerrey, Bob. When I Was a Young Man. New York: Harcourt, 2002.

Lucas, Adam. Going Home Again. Guilford, CT: Lyons Press, 2004.

Madden, Bill. Damned Yankees: A No-Holds-Barred Account of Life with "Boss Steinbrenner." New York: Warner Books, 1991.

Neuharth, Al. Confessions of an S.O.B. New York: Doubleday, 1989.

Olney, Buster. The Last Night of the Yankee Dynasty. New York: HarperCollins, 2004.

Osborne, Tom. What It Means to Be a Husker. Chicago: Triumph Books, 2004.

Prichard, Peter. The Making of McPaper: The Inside Story of USA TODAY. New York: Universal Press Syndicate, 1987.

Sayers, Gale, with Al Silverman. I Am Third. New York: The Viking Press, 1970.

Sayers, Gale. My Life and Times. Chicago: Triumph Books, 2007.

Veeck, Bill, and Ed Linn. Veeck as in Wreck. Chicago: University of Chicago Press, 1962.

Veeck, Mike, and Pete Williams. Fun Is Good. New York: Rodale Press, 2005.